ISLAM
AND
AMERICA

D0817245

ISLAM
AND
AMERICA

ANSWERS to the **31**
Most-Asked QUESTIONS

GEORGE BRASWELL

BROADMAN
&HOLMAN
PUBLISHERS

NASHVILLE TENNESSEE

Copyright © 2005
by George W. Braswell, Jr.
All rights reserved
Printed in the United States of America

Ten-Digit ISBN: 0–8054–2478–4
Thirteen-Digit ISBN: 978–0–8054–2478–2

Published by Broadman & Holman Publishers
Nashville, Tennessee

Dewey Decimal Classification: 297
Subject Heading: ISLAM / MUSLIMS

1 2 3 4 5 6 7 8 9 10 15 14 13 12 11 10 09 08 07 06 05

Contents

Why Write Such a Book?

Since September 11, 2001, the day of attack and terror and killings in the United States, Americans have asked many questions about the religion Islam and about Muslim peoples. Most Americans have not studied Islam in depth, have not lived among Muslim peoples in other lands and cultures for any amount of time, and have not engaged Muslims in many serious conversations.

Although Islam was introduced to the world in the Arabian peninsula in the seventh century after Jesus Christ, it has had an influential life across the world for some fourteen hundred years, and has grown in numbers and pervasive presence to 1.3 billion followers. Still, most Americans have remained disinterested and aloof from examining the religion.

Thus, since September 11, there has been a flurry of questions by Americans. Civic clubs like Lions and Rotary and Kiwanis invite speakers on Islam. University campuses sponsor lectures on Islam, and some require the entering first class to read the Qur'an. Churches hold workshops on Islam and Christian understandings of Islam and relations to Muslim peoples.

American mass media have included the comments of politicians, government leaders, Islamic spokespersons, academic scholars, terrorism experts, and Christian leaders. A number of books have steadily hit the bookstores on various subjects dealing with Islam.

Some have said that Islam is a peaceful religion. Some have said that only a few misled and misinformed Muslims have acted in violence. Some have said that Islam is being attacked and Muslims are being denigrated. Some have said that Islam is in a battle with the Judaic-Christian West for supremacy.

Americans are puzzled. And they ask questions. If Islam is a peaceful and freedom-loving religion, why is Saudi Arabia, the premier Sunni Muslim nation, such a seedbed of militant Islam, an Islam which castigates the Western Christian world and which grows up and sends its militants around the world to spread its ultraconservative Islam as well as wound and kill others whom it hates? If Islam is such a peaceful and freedom-loving religion, why has Iran, the premier Shiite Muslim nation, for the last twenty-five years under the aegis and influence of Ayatollah Khomeini launched its jihad across world cultures, often resulting in violence and death?

Often what Americans know about Islam is what they see in mass media and what they read in print about Islam in Saudi Arabia, Iran, Lebanon, the West Bank and Gaza, the happenings in Israel, the Sudan, Indonesia, Philippines, Afghanistan, Pakistan, Europe, and the United States. Thus, their questions are serious, and they seek answers that are understandable.

My Experience with Islam and Muslims

My first involved knowledge of Islam came as a student at the Divinity School of Yale University studying comparative religions during 1958–1961.

My firsthand knowledge and experience with Islam and Muslim peoples came when my family and I lived in Iran during 1968–1974. I was given the opportunity to teach English and comparative religions at the Faculty of Islamic Theology of the University of Teheran to several hundred Iranian Muslim students. The Faculty of Islamic Theology granted master and doctorate degrees to students in preparation to become high school and university teachers of Islam, to become clerics in mosques and other Islamic institutions, and to become chaplains in the armed services.

While working on MA and PhD degrees in cultural anthropology with specialization in Middle Eastern cultures and religions at the University of North Carolina at Chapel Hill from 1971 to 1975, I did original research in Iran on political and traditional Islam as expressed in the mosques, among Muslim clerics, and in society in general.

My teaching and research in Iran led me into visits and conversations in more than one hundred mosques with tens of ayatollahs and mullahs and other Muslims.

From 1974 until the present, I have taught at Southeastern Baptist Theological Seminary and recently as distinguished professor of missions and world religions. I have taken several thousand students to visit mosques and hold in-depth conversation with Muslim leaders in Washington, DC, New York City, Atlanta, and the Raleigh-Durham-Chapel Hill area of North Carolina.

Dr. Braswell's Ph.D. Class at Muslim University in Tehran, Iran

Dr. Braswell's Class with Imam Speaking in Mosque in Washington, DC

I have also researched Islam in mosques and among Muslim peoples during the last twenty years in Africa, the Middle East, Asia, and Europe.

Recent writings on Islam have included two books: *Islam: Its Prophet, Peoples, Politics, and Power* (1996) and *What You Need to Know about Islam and Muslims* (2000).

What Is Islam Trying to Tell Americans?

A Slumbering America Beginning to Awaken to Islam

When Ayatollah Khomeini established the Islamic Republic of Iran in 1979 and called America "the Great Satan," there was some notice in the American public that a religion named Islam was on the landscape. Shortly thereafter the United States Embassy in Teheran was taken over by "militant" Muslims, and Americans were held captive for 444 days. The Islamic terms *ayatollah* and *jihad* became everyday words in the mass media. Still there was little concern for understanding Islam among the American public.

The 1990s roared in with Islam becoming a center-stage attraction. Both large and small attacks by individuals in the names of Allah and Islam and jihad against American interests and Americans and others began to occur with some frequency.

The Attacks of a Pattern of Terror, Violence, and Killings That Awakened America— What Is Islam Trying to Tell Americans?

An emerging pattern of planned and well-coordinated attacks occurred in the 1990s against Americans and American interests both in the United States and abroad. The violence and killings were against American governmental and military

1

objects as well as American citizens and peoples of other nationalities and religions who happened to be in the way. Some of the attacks and killings included:

November 5, 1990
A Muslim Murders a Jew

New York: El-Sayyid Nosair, an Egyptian, killed a Jewish man, Meir Kahane, in the Marriott East Side Hotel in New York City after having trained for jihad with other Muslims in a shooting range on eastern Long Island.

February 26, 1993
Six Killed and One Thousand Wounded

New York: A car bomb was detonated at the World Trade Center, killing six and injuring a thousand with damages to the building of $510 million. Implicated were Ramzi Yousef, half Palestinian and half Pakistani, with the Muslim cleric, Sheikh Omar Rahman, head of the mosque in Jersey City, New Jersey, and other Muslims. Ramzi Yousef escaped and was later captured in Pakistan and brought back to the US for trial. Rahman is serving a life sentence in the United States. Ramzi had intended to bring down the Twin Towers.

January 7, 1995
Plotting to Kill Thousands

Manila, Philippines: Police found an apartment where Ramzi Yousef was making explosives to blow up twelve US 747s flying into America over the Pacific Ocean and to kill the Pope during his visit to Manila. Ramzi was later to be apprehended in Pakistan. Osama bin Laden's brother had paid the rent on the apartment. Ramzi had previously put explosives underneath a seat of a Philippine plane which blew up and killed a passenger.

June 26, 1996
Nineteen Killed and Four Hundred Wounded

Saudi Arabia: The Khobar Towers were truck-bombed, killing nineteen Americans and wounding four hundred in the US military housing complex. The bomb was the largest ever used in the Middle East against a US target.

February 22, 1998
Osama bin Laden Issued Statement to Kill Americans

Afghanistan: A statement was transmitted over mass media from Osama bin Laden that to kill Americans and their civilian and military allies is an individual duty for every Muslim who can do it in any country in which it is possible. Later was to follow his "Declaration of Jihad Against Jews and Christians."

Newly Constructed Mosque in
Johannesburg, South Africa, with
Aid from Saudi Arabia

August 7, 1998
Two Hundred and Twenty-four Killed and Five Thousand
Wounded

Nairobi and Dar es Salaam: The United States embassies in Nairobi, Kenya, and in Dar es Salaam, Tanzania, were truck-bombed almost simultaneously by assailants; two hundred and thirteen were killed in Nairobi and eleven in Dar es Salaam with the wounding of five thousand by terrorists associated with Osama bin Laden.

October 12, 2000
Seventeen Killed

Aden Harbor, Yemen: The *USS Cole* was attacked by a small boat with explosives in the Aden harbor, killing seventeen US seamen and nearly sinking the ship.

September 11, 2001
Three Thousand Killed and Untold Wounded

New York City Twin Towers, the Pentagon, and Pennsylvania: Between 7:45 a.m. and 8:42 a.m. on September 11, four planes took off from airports on the east coast with nineteen hijackers aboard—fifteen Saudi Arabs, two Emiratis, one Lebanese, and an Egyptian Arab named Mohammed Atta. Two planes were flown into the north and south towers of the World Trade Center. One plane was flown into the Pentagon. One plane crashed into a Pennsylvania field. Altogether about three thousand were killed, the worst attack ever upon United States peoples and soil, greater than that of Japan's attack at Pearl Harbor.

Before and after September 11, many terrorist attacks upon Americans and American interests worldwide and in the United States were prevented, and terrorists were apprehended.

Behind all of these attacks has been a voiced hatred against America by terrorist leaders and by suicide bombers implicitly and explicitly in the name of Islam and the God of Islam, Allah.

September 11, 2001: A Day of Infamy, Anger, and Beginning Resolve

Four hijacked planes out of Boston, Newark, and Washington crashed into the World Trade Center buildings, the Pentagon, and a field in Pennsylvania on Tuesday, September 11, 2001, killing about three thousand people of many ages and races and religions. Later evidence pointed to the deceased hijackers as nineteen men of Arab descent, fifteen of whom were natives of Saudi Arabia. Indications were that the Arab men were on a mission in the name of Allah and their religion, Islam. Mounting evidence provided information for the origin and inspiration of their mission, a jihad, supported by the Al-Qaeda terrorist network of Osama bin Laden.

America became angry and anxious and questioning about the reliance of the hijackers upon a religion that appeared to encourage such militancy and violence to wreak death and devastation upon Americans and visitors to its shores who happened to be in the places of attack that day.

Such violence by Islamic militants had been in the distant memory of America for several decades. A touchstone for America's memory was the rise of the Islamic Republic of Iran in 1979 under the leadership of Ayatollah Khomeini when the United States Embassy was taken over and its staff held hostage for 444 days. At that time Ayatollah Khomeini labeled America as "the Great Satan."

During the Persian Gulf crisis and the war of 1990–1991, Saddam Husain co-opted Islamic religious leaders in Iraq to declare a jihad against the immoral and corrupt and infidel America and its allies. Osama bin Laden, at the time of the United States-led war against the Taliban regime of Afghanistan in the fall of 2001 and the terrorists in the country, called for a jihad against the infidel America and its allies and for the killing of Americans wherever they could be found.

For the last twenty-five years, America has been the target in word and action of militant Muslims who in the name of Islam call for its destruction, castigating it as infidel, immoral, corrupt, and satanic, and worthy of a jihad against it. Thus, American soldiers and civilians have been killed; American embassies and other properties where they have been present have been attacked; and American ships and planes have been targeted with explosives.

Americans in general have not had much experience and relationships with Muslim peoples who practice their religion, Islam. The actions and words of militant Muslims have found visual images and harsh words in mass media print and television. After September 11, Americans were shown over mass media demonstrations of Muslims in streets around the world joyful of the terrorist attack.

Often, when Muslim leaders worldwide spoke about the attack, it was couched not in outrage against the perpetrators but in some sympathy that America deserved it because of the biases in its foreign policy and its dealings with the Muslim peoples. The wealthiest of the Saudi Arabian princes came to New York City to give the mayor a check for ten million dollars in the aftermath of the Twin Towers' destruction. When the prince stated that perhaps United States foreign policy had something to do with the attack, insinuating that America deserved it, the mayor returned the check to him.

Thus, Americans in their homes, on university campuses, in churches, in schools, and in civic clubs are asking questions about Islam as never before.

Questions Americans Are Asking

Americans are asking questions from what they see presented over mass media and from what they read. They are serious questions. They are sincere questions. Some of the questions Americans are asking:

- What is the religion Islam really like? Who are Muslims?
- Why did President Bush rapidly declare that Islam is a peaceful religion after September 11 when for several decades Islamic leaders from the Middle East to Asia and throughout Africa have stated hatred of and violence against America and Americans?
- Why is the word *jihad* so frequently used by Muslims? Does it mean to kill Muslims or non-Muslims?
- Why is terrorism associated with the religion Islam? Is militant Islam the same as jihadist Islam and political Islam? Are Muslims who blow themselves up or kill others martyrs of Allah? Do they go straight to heaven for their deeds? Is martyrdom a guarantee or a shortcut to heaven for the martyrs?
- Does Islam allow freedom of religion? Why does Saudi Arabia, a strong Muslim nation, disallow churches to be built on its soil? Why did the Taliban of Afghanistan destroy the historical statues of Buddha? When Christians are a minority in Muslim lands, why does it seem so often that they are restricted in their practices?
- Why does Islam treat those who leave the religion as apostates? Why do apostates face persecution or are outcast or killed? How does this practice fit with freedom of religion?
- When a Muslim nation calls itself an Islamic Republic, what does it mean? Does it rule in the name of Allah? Does it base its laws on the Qur'an and the Sharia law? How does an Islamic republic form of government relate to the concepts of democracy and freedom of speech and

freedom of religion? What is going on in Saudi Arabia, in Iran, in the Sudan, in Nigeria, and in Malaysia in their applications of Sharia law?

- Why do some Muslim women wear a veil and others do not? In Islam what are the guidelines for the relationships of a man and a woman and a husband and a wife? Why cannot Saudi Arabian women have a driver's license? Why are Muslim women segregated in the mosques and many other public places?

- Does Islam really teach hatred and violence toward Jews and Christians? Does Islam consider Judaism and Christianity corrupt religions?

- Is Allah of Islam the same God as the God of Christianity? Why do Muslims say that the Bible has been corrupted? Why does Islam deny the historical fact of the crucifixion of Jesus on a cross? Do Muslims believe that Jesus is just as important as Muhammad?

- What is Islam like in America? Is Louis Farrakhan the same kind of Muslim as Muhammad Ali and Ayatollah Khomeini and Yassir Arafat and the Wahhabi royal family of Saudi Arabia and Wallace D. Muhammad?

- Is there historical and contemporary confrontation between Islam and the West and between Islam and Christianity? Have Islam and Christianity been able to get along during fourteen hundred years of encounters? Is Islam such a superior system in the minds of Muslims that any other religion or political system or cultural pattern is inferior and doomed to failure?

Islam Has Specific Sources of Answers to These Questions

Americans are becoming more aware that Islam seems to be monolithic in some areas and diverse in others. They know that the largest populated Muslim nation is Indonesia, which tends to practice freedom of religion. They also are learning that Saudi Arabia, with nearly 100 percent of its people Muslim, practices an ultraconservative kind of Islam known as Wahhabism. Wahhabism dispenses justice in cutting off hands for stealing and heads for adultery and views the worldviews and values of the Western world, of Judaism, and of Christianity as materialistic, corrupt, immoral, and evil.

Regardless of differences within Islam, certain specific authorities are foundational to Islam and the beliefs and practices of Muslims. They are as follows:

- The **Qur'an**, the sacred scripture of Islam, is the foundational and supreme authority.
- The **Hadith**, the sayings and deeds of the prophet Muhammad, is the second most important authority.
- The **Sharia**, the body of laws and legal interpretations, is a key reference for jurisprudence.
- The practice of **Ijtihad**, a consensus upon a matter by scholarly Muslim leadership, is another source for settling matters which affect Muslims.
- The practice of **Qiyas**, the use of analogical reasoning by Muslim scholars, is employed as a means for ascertaining answers for Muslim thought and practice.

Muslims insist that all their thought and practice must be based on the primary sources of the Qur'an and the Hadith. Since these sources were given first in the Arabic language, it is essential that scholars and interpreters use Arabic as the language to decipher the truths from these documents. Various schools of Sharia developed early in Islam, which may have differing opinions and interpretations. However, Sharia must never contradict the Qur'an and the Hadith.

Although Islam does not have an official ordained clergy, categories of Muslim authorities and leaders (the Ulama) are qualified through years of study and research and writing. The people look to them for guidance on all matters of thought and

behavior. These leaders carry the specific titles of imam, ayatollah, sheikh, and other localized titles.

Dr. Braswell with Imam in African American Mosque in Washington, DC

CHAPTER 1

What Is the Religion Islam Really Like?

Who Are Muslims?

Mass Media Images of Muslims and Islam

The American public has seen Muslims portrayed over television in various ways. Anwar Sadat, former president of Egypt, who was assassinated by a militant Islamic group in Cairo, was seen as a praying man. Sadat led a war against Israel and also entered a peace agreement with Israel.

Ayatollah Khomeini, the turbaned leader who chased out the Western-leaning shah and established the Islamic Republic of Iran, was viewed by many Muslims around the world as the great Muslim revolutionary who would give Islam superior status in the world. Americans saw him portrayed over mass media as a stern old man who castigated America as satanic, corrupt, and immoral, who supported Islamic jihad movements around the world, and who issued a death sentence upon the head of the novelist Salman Rushdie who wrote *The Satanic Verses*.

Osama bin Laden has been labeled the leader of the Al-Qaeda terrorist organization who has launched strikes against American targets around the world. In mass media he has issued statements against many entities including America,

Jews, and Christians and urged his agents as well as Muslims worldwide to kill Americans and others in the name of Allah and Islam.

Wallace D. Muhammad, the son of Elijah Muhammad who founded the Nation of Islam in America, is portrayed in the mass media as transforming his former American Muslim Mission into an orthodox expression of Islam in the United States. Louis Farrakhan, leader of the current Nation of Islam, is seen in the mass media as a fiery speaker who views Elijah Muhammad as a deity, courts Islamic revolutionary leaders from around the world, and continues a running attack upon Jews and Christians.

Seldom does the American public see the life of a Muslim living in a city or small village who raises a family, provides food for the family, works for a living, yearns for the education of his children, tends to aging parents, says prayers daily, and looks for a better life.

Islam: A Required and Certain Straight Path

The core of Islam, according to the Qur'an and the Hadith, is its required and prescribed set of beliefs and practices. These beliefs are nonnegotiable and provide the worldview of all Muslims. These practices are regular and orderly and also nonnegotiable. They follow an exact calendar of daily, monthly, and yearly rituals and ceremonies.

Islam means "submission." *Muslim* means "one who submits." Islam is a religion of submission to Allah and the truths and practices enunciated in the Qur'an and in the Hadith as clarified by various legal systems and rulings by Islamic specialists. Islam is a religion of the "straight path" (Qur'an 1:6). The path has few deviations and curves in terms of its major beliefs and practices. Whether you are an American Muslim or an Indonesian Muslim or a Saudi Arabian Muslim or President

Sadat or Osama bin Laden, the straight path of Islam is the same in the Qur'anic prescriptions.

Required Beliefs from the Qur'an

Five major beliefs are:

Monotheism: belief in one deity, Allah, who shares his nature with no one or anything.

Angels: Gabriel brings the revelations from Allah to Muhammad, which are codified in the Qur'an.

Scriptures: The Qur'an is the final and perfect revelation of Allah which corrects the Torah and Injil.

Prophets: Muhammad is the final prophet of Allah who brings the correct revelation.

Day of judgment: There is a final day of judgment when Allah metes out rewards and punishments.

1. **Islam is a monotheistic religion.** It believes in one deity whose name is Allah. The first chapter of the Qur'an, known as the Fatiha or "opening," summarizes what Muslims believe about Allah. Allah is most gracious and merciful, sustainer of the world, and master of the day of judgment. He is to be worshipped, and his aid is to be sought (Qur'an 1:1–7). The Qur'an requires that Allah be called by his beautiful names though it does not list them all (Qur'an 59:22–24). The Qur'an states that Allah will not forgive idolatry and regards the most heinous sin (shirk) as ascribing partners with Allah. Islam condemns the Christian view of Jesus as expressed in the doctrine of the trinity. Thus the central concept of deity for Islam is the unity of Allah (*Tawhid*).

2. **Angels are a prominent belief of Islam.** They are beings who carry out the commands of Allah (Qur'an 2:285; 6:100; 34:40–41; 46:29–32; 72:1–28). The archangel Gabriel is the most famous angel who appeared to Muhammad and brought the Qur'an to him to recite. Other angels include Michael, who gives providence and is guardian of the Jews; Israfil, who

summons to resurrection; and Izrail, the angel of death. Islamic Hadith (tradition) teaches that two angels are assigned to each individual at birth. One records good deeds, and the other records the bad. The angels give the individual's accountability at judgment day. Allah has created other spiritual beings called "jinn" with freedom of choice for good or evil. Some Islamic scholars consider Satan an angel, and others consider him a jinn.

3. The Qur'an states that prophets have been sent to peoples of the world with the same message from Allah in heaven (Qur'an 2:38, 177, 252, 285; 4:80, 164; 18:110; 33:40; 17:70). It emphasizes that there is no difference in the messages of the prophets including Moses and Jesus (Qur'an 2:136). The Qur'an mentions some twenty-five prophets by name. Muhammad is the final prophet (Qur'an 33: 40, 45–46). Islamic tradition indicates 124,000 prophets. Jesus is mentioned ninety-seven times in the Qur'an and referred to as Messiah, word of Allah, spirit of Allah, born of the Virgin Mary, and worker of miracles. The Qur'an states that Jesus was no more than a messenger like those before him. Islam does not believe that Jesus was crucified on a cross or that he was raised from the tomb.

4. Islam believes that the Qur'an contains the very words of Allah and that the "mother of the book" is with Allah in heaven (Qur'an 85:21–22; 43:3–4; 13:39). Traditional Islam views the Qur'an as a miracle, an uncreated word or book, given in the Arabic language. Therefore, literary or historical criticism is not acceptable. It is composed of 114 chapters or suras and 6,616 verses or ayas, and 77,934 words. From the night the angel Gabriel came to Muhammad with the words to recite the Qur'an in AD 610 until Muhammad's death in AD 632, the Qur'an was given. By AD 652 the Qur'an was canonized as the authorized version. Muslims believe it contains guidance for all matters of life. They memorize it, recite it, and create artistic expressions from it. The Qur'an refers to other scriptures such as the Torah and the Injil (Gospel) which Allah gave to the Jews through the prophet Moses and to the Christians through the prophet Jesus. However, Islam believes that these scriptures were corrupted through various translations and interpretations and that the Qur'an is the final perfect expression of Allah's revelations.

5. A day of judgment resulting in rewards in paradise or hell is described in the Qur'an. As Allah created all, so Allah judges all. Judgment day is described variously as a day of wrath, decision, truth, and retribution. The final hour will come suddenly. There are scenes of apocalyptic doom with natural disasters and graves being opened (Qur'an 75; 82; 84). At judgment day each individual will stand before Allah where a scroll will be brought out for an accounting of all deeds (Qur'an 17:13–14). Paradise is a place of great delight to enjoy the presence of Allah and also to have sensual and sexual delight (Qur'an 3:14–15; 47:15; 55). Hell is described as a burning and odious place of boiling brains and molten lead poured into ears. It is the abode of idolaters, unbelievers, and the unrepentant (Qur'an 14:50; 76:4).

Various Islamic traditions refer to the return of Muhammad and Jesus at the judgment day to assist Allah in matters related to the final journeys to paradise and hell. A Sunni Muslim tradition tells of the return of Jesus as Messiah. He breaks the cross, kills all pigs, dies, and is buried beside Muhammad. The eschatological figure in Islam is called the Mahdi, the one to return and bring the world to judgment and Satan to submission.

Required Practices of the Qur'an

Some scholars write of the five pillars or practices of Islam. Some scholars write of the six major practices of Islam which include jihad. Six of the major practices are:

A confession (*Shahada*): There is no deity but Allah, and Muhammad is the messenger of Allah.

Financial giving (*zakat*): Muslims must contribute a certain percentage of their resources to Islam.

Prayers (*salat*): There are five stated formal prayers and other informal prayers (*Doa*).

Fasting (*Ramadan*): Muslims fast one month of each year from dawn to dusk.

Pilgrimage (*hajj*): Islam requires each Muslim to make a pilgrimage to Mecca once in a lifetime.

Holy Efforts (*jihad*): Muslims are to please Allah individually and collectively through the first five practices listed above and through holy warfare (another form of jihad) if called upon by an Islamic authority.

1. **The great confession (*Shahada*) of Islam is composed of seven Arabic words, "*Ilaha illa Allah. Muhammad rasul Allah.*"** "There is no deity but Allah. Muhammad is the messenger of Allah" (Qur'an 3:81; 5:83–84; 2:255; 3:18; 3:144; 4:87; 7:172; 33:40; 48:29; 64:8). Muslims believe that when these words are said, one is converted to Islam and it makes a Muslim a Muslim. These words are whispered in the ears of a newborn child. The confession is uttered daily in the formal prayers. It is said numerous times a day and during the last funeral ceremonies. The confession states the fullness of Islam in that it is based on monotheism and the prophethood of Muhammad.

2. **The giving of one's resources to Islam is known as almsgiving (*zakat*) and is required by the Qur'an** (Qur'an 2:43, 83, 110, 177, 277; 9:60, 103; 24:56; 27:3; 57:7; 59:7; 98:5). Zakat is 2.5 percent of one's wealth. The monies are used for building and supporting mosques, for printing Qur'ans, for the education of children in Qur'anic schools, and for worldwide missionary programs. Muslims may give an endowment (*waqf*) in money or property to build mosques, libraries, hospitals, and schools. Islam teaches that one is a trustee of Allah's creation and that giving purifies one's soul.

3. **Muslims are known around the world for their five daily stated prayers.** They must be voiced in Arabic. They may be done individually or in community, usually in a mosque. They must face in the direction of Mecca. The words and gestures are highly specific as Muslims line up in orderly rows. Men and women are segregated. The Qur'an requires that they be accomplished just as it states (Qur'an 2:3, 117; 11:114; 17:78; 20:14, 130; 30:17–18). The five prayers are said between dawn and sunrise, noon and mid-afternoon, mid-afternoon to sunset, sunset to twilight, and from twilight to dawn. A ritual washing is required of parts of the face, hands, and feet before each prayer. A leader called an imam stands before the people in the mosque, and they emulate his words and movements. Also, there are informal, extemporaneous prayers (*doa*) which serve as petitions, pleas, and praises to Allah, as well as for some Muslim groups to Islamic heroes and saint types. These may be voiced in one's native language.

4. **The Qur'an requires fasting of all Muslims unless there is a health problem at the time** (Qur'an 2:183–185). It is held during Ramadan, the ninth month of the Islamic lunar calendar. The calendar varies from year to year so that the fasting season will rotate seasonally. Fasting must be observed from sunrise to sunset, during which time there is no eating, drinking, frivolity, or sexual intercourse. After sunset and before dawn meals may be taken. The festival of Id Fitr (breaking the fast) is held at the end of Ramadan as a time of celebration for adhering to the fast and its meaning for physical and spiritual life. Large gatherings around meals and gift giving are part of the celebration.

5. **The pilgrimage (*hajj*) to Mecca is required by the Qur'an for every man and woman who is physically and financially able to go at least once in a lifetime** (Qur'an 2:196–201; 3:97; 22:26–29). Mecca is the holiest city of Islam. It is the birthplace of Muhammad. It is the city faced by over one

billion Muslims in their daily prayers. Tradition associates
Abraham and his son, Ishmael, with the city where they built an
altar (*Ka'bah*) for the worship of Allah. The religion of Abraham
was corrupted by Arab tribes. Muhammad later removed the
360 idols of the *Ka'bah* and instituted it as a place of worship for
Muslims to Allah. Some two million Muslims each year make
the pilgrimage where they perform ceremonies around the
Ka'bah and mosque and in the near vicinity of Mecca. Some pilgrims travel two hundred miles to the north of Mecca to the
second most sacred city of Islam, Medina, where Muhammad
established his first Muslim community (*Ummah*), built the first
mosque, and was laid to rest in a special tomb in AD 632. Only
Muslims are allowed to enter Mecca.

6. **Jihad is a prominent part of Islam** (Qur'an 2:244; 9:5;
9:29; 22:78; 47:4; 49:15). It has two meanings. The basic meaning is "to struggle or to strive" to fulfill the straight path for
which the Qur'an calls. It is the battle waged by a Muslim
against sin and disobedience and for observing all the practices
of Islam. A second meaning of *jihad* is the traditional holy war
waged against the enemies of Allah and Islam. Thus, jihad is
both a personal and a community commitment to defend and
spread the religion Islam by the tongue, by the heart, by the
hand, and if necessary by the sword. Tradition approves of violence against infidels and unbelievers and those who leave their
native religion in apostasy. The Qur'an promises to the martyr
(*shahid*) in battle a place in paradise and an honorable name
bestowed upon one's family (Qur'an 47:4–5).

CHAPTER 2

Why Is the Word *Jihad* Used So Frequently by Muslims?

Does *Jihad* Mean "to Kill Non-Muslims"?

What Does Jihad Have to Do with Peace?

Jihad in the Mass Media

Americans have heard of frequently in the mass media during the past thirty-five years. When television and print media present the news or stories on Islam, often it is in the context of militant and violent jihad.

When the Palestinian Liberation Organization (PLO) began in the 1960s, it protested the legitimacy of the nation of Israel and waged war against it with its military wing of operations. Much of the violence was sanctioned by jihad in the name of Allah.

Other Islamic militant groups such as the Muslim Brotherhood, Islamic Jihad, Hezbollah, and Hamas have waged military action against Israel, as well as against their own governments, often in the name of a jihad of Allah. Hamas in particular has sent suicide bombers into Israel, declaring them as martyrs of Allah and thus a part of the jihad of Islam.

Ayatollah Khomeini chased out the "corrupt and Western puppet" regime of the shah of Iran and established the Islamic Republic of Iran. The ayatollah called America "the Great Satan," supported the seizure of the United States Embassy in Teheran and held Americans hostage, and declared a jihad against neighboring Iraq and fought an eight-year war (1980–1988) against his Muslim neighbor in which hundreds of thousands of lives were lost with the promise of rewards of paradise to the martyrs. He declared a jihad against Salman Rushdie, author of *The Satanic Verses*, and offered a reward for his death.

Saddam Husain of Iraq, at the time of the Persian Gulf War, had his clerics declare a jihad against the United States and its allies. Osama bin Laden, leader of Al-Qaeda, called for a jihad against the United States, the Western world, corrupt rulers of Muslim peoples, and Jews and Christians. During the war against Iraq (2003), clerics in Iraq declared a jihad against the evil force of the United States and its allied invaders.

The recent writings of noted revolutionary Muslim thinkers such as al-Banna, Sayyid Qutb, and al-Mawdudi have inspired many to bring change into their Muslim societies. Noted Muslim clerics have preached jihadist sermons from their pulpits in the mosques. Islamic schools (*madrasa*) have taught jihadist curricula to young Muslim minds. Jihad has been a primary weapon for change.

In recent American experience, jihad has come to be known as the killing of Americans on both their home soil and places abroad. Muslim guests from countries such as Saudi Arabia, Pakistan, and Egypt have lived among Americans for a while and then have committed a jihad against them.

Thus, in America's knowledge and perception of Islam, the term *jihad* has become very prominent. Its meaning is little known except for how mass media present it in times of war and violence. Jihad in this context is not associated with peace.

What Is Jihad?

Classical Islamic teachings divide the world into two spheres. There is the sphere or way of heedlessness or ignorance or corruption and immorality or war known as Dar al-Harb. People in this sphere are not in submission to Allah and the straight path. Then there is the sphere of submission to Allah known as Dar al-Islam. This sphere includes Muslims who submit to Allah and follow the straight path of correct beliefs and practices. Thus, humans have two choices: to submit or to be in disobedience.

The mission (*daw'ah*) of Islam is to deal with the sphere of disobedience, ignorance, and war and bring the peoples of this sphere into Islam through conversion, capitulation, or coercion and either be a part of the Dar al-Islam or to live under it with restrictions. Jihad is the way to accomplish this mission either peacefully or sometimes violently.

Jihad has two basic meanings in Islam. The basic meaning, sometimes called "greater jihad," is "to struggle or to strive" to submit to and obey Allah in all the prescriptions in the Qur'an and the Hadith and the Sharia. This jihad is the personal struggle each Muslim wages against sin and all that is against Allah. It is also the mission to carry Islam to the world. The Qur'an urges the Muslim to stay on the straight path and to strive in Allah's cause (Qur'an 22:78; 49:15).

Another meaning of *jihad* is the traditional battle or war waged in the name of Allah against the enemies of Allah and Islam. It is referred to as "lesser jihad." This type of jihad needs a special declaration by a Muslim authority that Allah and Islam have been attacked or harmed to such an extent that military and violent action are necessary. Then, an Islamic-recognized authority can solicit and send an army or individuals on a jihad against the stated enemy.

The Qur'an in various places and times commands Muslims to fight for the cause of Allah and kill pagans wherever they are found. When meeting unbelievers, believers are urged to smite their necks and fight those who do not believe in Allah and the last day (Qur'an 2:244; 47:4; 9:5; 9:29). The Qur'an states that fighting is prescribed for Muslims although they may dislike it (Qur'an 2:216, 190). The Qur'an threatens one who does not fight with severe punishments at judgment day (Qur'an 9:81–82).

Rewards are promised to those who fight for Allah whether they are killed or victorious (Qur'an 4:74). A martyr (*shahid*) in jihad is guaranteed a place in paradise and an honorable name bestowed upon one's family (Qur'an 47:4–5; 48:16–17).

Both the Qur'an and the Hadith (sayings and deeds of Muhammad) approve of violence against infidels and other enemies of Allah. A Hadith reports that Muhammad was asked which deed is dearest to Allah. He replied in an order of preference to offer prayers at their fixed times, to be good and dutiful to one's parents, and to participate in jihad (religious warfare) in Allah's cause. Fighting and killing are described as beloved activities. Jihad is presented as coercive and violent. Muslims understand it to be an effort or struggle to bring righteousness and peace on earth. The history of Islam has revealed it to be warfare against tribes, peoples, persons, and nations whom Islam considers to be its enemies.

Jihad: When and Where

Muslims may refer to jihad in the four following ways:
1. Jihad of the tongue: speaking about their faith
2. Jihad of the hand: expressing their faith in good works
3. Jihad of the heart: making their faith a force for good

4. Jihad of the sword: defending their faith when under attack

The classical doctrine of jihad has come from the Islamic foundations of:

- Qur'anic prescriptions
- Hadith sayings and deeds of Muhammad
- Practices of the first four Caliphs (AD 632–661)
- Legal and jurisprudence rulings of Islamic law (*Sharia*)

Jihad then is the method to persuade, coerce, subdue, and tolerate non-Muslims until Islam is accepted and established. Historically, both Jews and Christians, called "People of the Book" by the Qur'an and Islam, have been given special status of limited toleration as non-Muslims. Jews and Christians have been required to pay certain special taxes; they have the freedom of worship in their synagogues and churches with restrictions

Islamic Cafeteria
in Singapore

upon proselytism and the enlargement of their properties for growth and prohibitions from time to time upon their service in the ranks of the military or high government positions.

How Islam Deals with the Issues of War and Peace

Some Examples of Literature with References to Peace and War

When the indexes of various literature on Islam are reviewed, it is interesting what is found about peace and war. In the index of *The Meaning of the Holy Qur'an* by Abdullah Yusuf Ali, the references to peace are the following:

- "The greeting of the righteous" (Qur'an 7:46; 10:10; 14:23; 36:58)
- "Incline toward peace" (Qur'an 8:61)
- "Salam as peace" (Qur'an 19:62)
- "Peace as tranquility" (Qur'an 11:26; 48:4, 18, 26)

In Ali's index, there is only one reference about war, which is "war against Allah" found in Qur'an 5:33–34. It describes the punishment for waging war against Allah and Muhammad to include execution or crucifixion or cutting off of hands and feet from opposite sides or exile.

In the four volume *The Oxford Encyclopedia of the Modern Islamic World*, edited by John Esposito, there is no separate topic for peace, and for the topic on war, one is referred to the headings of Fitnah, Ghazw, Jihad, and Military Forces.

In the index of the popular book *A Muslim Primer*, written by Ira G. Zepp Jr. and commended by Muslim scholars, there is no mention of peace or war.

In the 776-page book *Commandments by God in the Quran*, compiled by Nazar Mohammad, especially for Western readers of Islam, there is no mention of peace in the topics in the table of contents. There are several topics on "Striving" and jihad and a topic on "Defense" which includes war.

Intertwining of Peace and War: Not One without the Other

John Kelsay in his book *Islam and War* observes that in the classical Islamic tradition the obligation of believers (Muslims) is to strive for peace with justice. Peace is the predominance of al-Islam, which is submission to the will of God. Kelsay notes that believers must therefore think in terms of an obligation to establish a social order in which the priority of Islam is recognized. Then peace is the goal of life; justice, the form of peace; and an Islamic social order provides the security for all humanity within the providence of God.

Kelsay points out the worldview of classical Islam which divides the human condition into two spheres: that of heedlessness and ignorance (*al-Harb*), which is the territory of war and that of submission to Allah (*al-Islam*) which is the territory of Islam or peace. This territory of Islam is a political entity that affirms the supremacy of Islamic values.

The territory of Islam is usually presided over by a leader who is knowledgeable of the Qur'an and Hadith to make governing judgments and who may rely upon Islamic religious scholars for advice. It provides for religious pluralism in the sense of protected minorities (*dhimmi*) who may have relative freedom by paying taxes and submitting to the Islamic authorities.

Thus, the classical Islamic view of peace is when the community of Muslims (*ummah*) has either through education or missionary activity brought non-Muslims out of the sphere of war into the sphere of submission to Allah and the sphere of peaceful Islamic values and society. Until the sphere of Islam has been established, there is a state of war within the lives of the unbelievers who are heedless and ignorant. There is the obligation of Muslims to establish the true Islamic world.

Islam Views War Only for Defense Purposes

The Islamic view of war is for defense purposes. Islam is never the aggressor. Its task is to invite, educate, and encourage non-Muslims to come to Islam. However, to use force in the name of Allah and Islam could extend the territory of Islam and establish peace.

Islam has rules for governing the use of war and waging war. Islam has waged war when a non-Islamic political entity refused to accept the sovereignty of Islam by not converting or by refusing to pay the required tax to the Islamic authority. The Islamic authority must study the need for force, examine the classical and historical documents, and then make a decision to call a military jihad and summon adult males for duty. And the war must be conducted according to Islamic values in the path of Allah and not for booty and personal gain.

Newly Constructed Mosque in
Capetown, South Africa, with Aid
from Iran

John Kelsay raises the question which has arisen out of recent militant Islam: What does the Islamic tradition say about military action on the part of individual citizens, militia groups, that is, "soldiers without portfolio"? Classical Islam has held that a competent and right authority only has the power to call for a militant jihad or war. The question is asked about the authority of militant groups such as Islamic Jihad, Hezbollah, Hamas, Muslim Brotherhood, and Al-Qaeda and its derivatives. Under whose authority do they operate, and is it legitimate within Islam?

Kelsay concludes his section on peace by writing that "Islam by its nature is interested in politics. It is, by tradition and historic experience, interested in the creation and preservation of a political entity that in some sense reflects Islamic values. It is, to put it another way, interested not just in the avoidance of conflict but in the creation of a just society. That, I think, is the conclusion to which a consideration of the Islamic view of peace leads."

In many political entities or nations where there is a Muslim majority, there is an attempt by Muslim groups to have governance by Islamic law (*Sharia*). Nigeria, the largest populated nation in Africa, and Pakistan, the fourth largest Muslim nation worldwide, have faced the question of establishing Sharia for their legal systems. Saudi Arabia, Iran, Sudan, and Malaysia demonstrate the use of Sharia legal systems. Egypt has faced dissident and revolutionary Muslim thinkers and activists who have had followings demanding governance based on Islamic institutions and values. The recent Taliban regime in Afghanistan enforced regulations of Sharia upon the women especially.

Kenneth Cragg, noted scholar of Islam and missiologist, wrote in *A Future with Islam* of the inherently political nature of Islam. He asserted that Islam "believes itself commissioned with a mandate of power to institutionalize divine sovereignty on earth via the Sharia, the ummah and the dawah (sacred law, community, and state). If the Qur'an is the perfect road map for individual and community living, and if the example of the prophet Muhammad in his sayings and deeds is the par excellent model, and if Muhammad's establishment of the nation-state in Medina under his leadership as prophet, patriarch, political and legal ruler, and commander in chief is the way in the 'straight path,' then peace is best achieved under Islam. If at times war is necessary to accomplish the establishment of peace with justice, then Islam provides for it also in the 'straight way.'"

The Great Shah Mosque
in Isfahan, Iran

CHAPTER 3

Why Is Terrorism
Associated with Islam?

Is Anyone Protected from the
Violence of Martyrs?

Are Muslim Martyrs
Guaranteed Heaven?

Words and Weapons Hurled at Americans
by Muslim Terrorists

Since the Ayatollah Khomeini of Iran called America "the Great Satan" in his revolution beginning in 1979, Americans have been the targets of vitriolic words and violent acts and continuous threats of Muslim terrorists in the name of Islam and Allah. America's close relationship with Israel has drawn fire from terrorists and other strong Muslim voices. Terrorists and other voices have criticized America's lack of attention and support of Palestinian causes. Terrorists have criticized America's favoritism toward Muslim "secular and Western-oriented" heads of state in Muslim lands.

America has been singled out as a colonialist, imperialist, power-hungry nation which desires to establish its empire around the world in arrogance and control. Also, America has been called a corrupt, immoral, and disbelieving nation. Jews and Christians, in particular, have been targeted by the terrorist organization, Al-Qaeda, as an immoral and infidel people who should not be allowed to corrupt Muslim lands and holy places.

The result of Muslim terrorists has been the loss and maimed life of thousands of Americans and other nationals in terrorist bombings, many of them suicidal bombers. The greatest single loss of life occurred on September 11, 2001, with the attacks on the World Trade Center and the Pentagon.

Who Are Muslim Terrorists and Why Are They So?

Some would argue that someone's terrorist is another's liberation fighter. Dictionaries define *terrorism* as "unlawful acts of violence." It may be against individuals, groups, or governments. Muslim terrorism has resulted in acts of extreme violence in taking the lives of both Muslims and Americans and other individuals into the thousands. And Muslim terrorism relies on its legitimacy on Islamic sources.

Terrorists recite chapters and verses of the Qur'an to justify their violence and killings. They point to their prophet Muhammad who led militias in battles under the aegis of the favor of Allah in the slaying of tribes and individuals to establish Islam and the ummah. They align themselves with Islamic history in the rule of the great caliphs and warfare in establishing Islamic empires headquartered in Mecca, Damascus, Baghdad, Cairo, Cordova, and Constantinople. They pride themselves on following the legal and legitimate commands (*fatwas*) of Islamic scholars and jurists and clerics when they declare jihad against an enemy.

Muslim terrorists rely on the concept and practice of jihad. Jihad has been presented earlier in chapter 2. Militant jihad is based on the Qur'an and the example of the prophet Muhammad and on Islamic tradition. Terrorists loudly and proudly state that they do their violent deeds in the name of Allah and for the furtherance of Islam. They see the world as neatly divided between *we* and *they,* between the superior religion of Islam and the ignorant views and lifestyles of others, and between the true believers and the infidels.

Do the Qur'an and the prophet Muhammad condone terrorism? The Qur'an and Muhammad do not define terrorism. They present jihad and the conditions upon which it may be practiced. If jihad is "religiously sanctioned warfare," there are rules and regulations for its expression. The use of violence is usually condoned to combat injustice. A regulation in Islamic law concerning warfare is noncombatant immunity. Thus, the kind of terrorism that includes attacking small children, women, and aged men is prohibited by the traditions of Islamic law.

Gold Domed Mosque of the Imam
in Meshad, Iran

How are Allah and Islam used to justify terrorism through violent acts, hijackings, and hostage taking? Basic to the Muslim terrorist mind-set is the understanding that Islam is the superior religion, that the community-nation-state (*ummah*) which Muhammad established in Medina (AD 622–632) and which the first four caliphs (AD 632–661) who followed him further developed is the "straight path" for the ideal and perfect society. Ayatollah Khomeini and other Muslim leaders have justified militant actions against Satan's evil forces, namely America and secular Muslim leaders like Saddam Husain, who oppose Allah. Osama bin Laden justified his violence and killings on the Qur'an and the Hadith. Desperate Muslim terrorists, educated and inspired by Muslim revolutionary writers and fiery Muslim clerics, use the Qur'an and the Islamic traditions to justify militant acts. The Hadith is used to justify violent actions by the terrorists saying, "Muhammad did it, approved it, or did not oppose it."

Does Islam permit suicide bombers? The Muslim terrorists who hijacked the aircraft and flew them into buildings on September 11, 2001, killed innocent noncombatants, including Muslims. Therefore, some scholars would argue that the action was prohibited (*haram*) by Islam. Also, some would assert that there was no legitimate authority and no clerical ruling (*fatwa*) to condone such acts. Suicide bombers have been taught and have been trained to explode devices on their bodies to wreak violence and death on others. Their martyrdom, not called suicide by them and their teachers, merits for them immediate entrance into paradise. Some Islamic authorities argue that both from the Qur'an and from Hadith there is a severe penalty for a Muslim to take his own life. Hell is the reward for suicide. Thus, to take one's life is to disobey and turn from the path of Islam.

Why do some Muslims seem so violent? Muslims come under the influence of authoritarian and repressive governments who use violence, repression, and terror against the people. So news comes from Muslim populations about battles between government and themselves. Since World War II, many Muslims have been inspired by the revolutionary writers in Egypt, Iran, and Pakistan, urging an Islamic state and the revival and resurgence of Islam. The history of Islam also has many acts of violence in it, including the violent death of many of its leaders, both Sunni and Shia, and violence in its beginning under Muhammad as commander in chief of the Muslim militias that battled tribes for power and position, including Jewish tribes. It is asserted that Muhammad led his troops into twenty-seven battles and sent them into thirty-nine other battles. However, most Muslims are not terrorists, nor do they participate in violent activities.

Do Muslims and Islamic organizations support terrorism? Some Muslims individually and collectively support terrorist activities. Muslims who submit themselves under the preaching and guidance of a Muslim cleric like an ayatollah who may preach violence against infidel nations and infidel peoples may be influenced to give support and aid which results in the violence of terrorism. Some Qur'anic schools (*madrasa*) teach the youth about militant jihad and the violence of terrorism and serve as recruiting grounds for terrorists. Some mosques led by firebrand Muslim clerics serve as breeding grounds for terrorism. Examples of these have been found found in many places including Pakistan, Saudi Arabia, Afghanistan, the Gaza Strip, Lebanon, Indonesia, Philippines, Europe, and the state of New Jersey (USA).

Do Muslims hate non-Muslims? Do Muslims hate America? Certainly terrorists hate America and Americans because they kill them—women, aged men, children, and Americans of all religions. Some Muslims are taught that non-Muslims are infidels and are to be shunned. Some Muslims are taught that America is a crusader nation following the example of the medieval crusades to control and subdue the Islamic nations and the Muslim peoples. Some Muslims hate America for its foreign policy toward Palestinians and other Muslim peoples, which they think is biased against them. However, many Muslims send their children to study in the United States, visit America, and admire the freedoms and democratic ideals which characterize Americans. And many Muslims welcome friendships with Americans and the opportunity to host them in their homes.

Why was Salman Rushdie condemned to death for authoring *The Satanic Verses*? Ayatollah Khomeini issued a formal legal opinion (*fatwa*) in February 1989 to sentence to death Salman Rushdie.

In the name of God Almighty; there is only one God,
to whom we shall all return; I would like to inform all
the intrepid Muslims in the world that the author of
the book entitled *The Satanic Verses* which has been
compiled, printed and published in opposition to

**Dr. Braswell Engages Muslim
leader and Followers at Mosque in
Nairobi, Kenya**

Islam, the Prophet, and the Koran, as well as those publishers who were aware of its contents, have been sentenced to death. I call on all zealous Muslims to execute them quickly, wherever they find them, so that no one will dare insult the Islamic sanctions. Whoever is killed on this path will be regarded as a martyr, God willing. In addition, anyone who has access to the author of the book, but does not possess the power to execute him, should refer him to the people so that he may be punished for his actions. May God's blessing be on you all.

Rushdie, a native of India and a resident of Great Britain, was accused by a noted Islamic cleric-scholar of defiling and opposing Islam, Muhammad, and the Qur'an. Rushdie's book was a novel. A bounty was placed on his head. Muslims protested and rioted against Rushdie and his book in several countries.

Does Islam promote martyrdom? The word for *martyr* is *shahid*, which comes from the word for the confession (*shahada*) in Islam, which is that there is no deity but Allah and Muhammad is his messenger. The word *martyr* is not in the Qur'an, but virtue and jihad in submission to Allah are encouraged (Qur'an 85:3–8; 4:69; 2:154). In Qur'an 47:4–6, it is stated that for those Muslims in battle against the unbelievers who are killed, Allah will never let their deeds be lost and will admit them into paradise. The Hadith literature strongly promotes martyrdom, and Muhammad in several traditions encourages martyrs and promises them the greatest of rewards in paradise. Muslim terrorists and suicide bombers have left behind evidence of videos and writings in which they fully expected that their martyrdom would result in Allah's granting them paradise and all its delights.

For centuries Muslim men have been promised the sexual favors of the *huri*, virgin females, in paradise, especially if they are martyrs on behalf of Allah and the cause of Islam. Lately some writers have been defining *huri* to mean "raisins," not female virgins.

Thus, do the Qur'an and Islamic traditions and legal systems justify acts of terrorism and violence as seen in suicidal bombings, killing of innocents in marketplaces, businesses, streets, on public buses, and the embassies of countries in both Muslim and non-Muslims lands?

It depends on which Muslims one listens to, on which Qur'anic verses are recited, and on which Islamic tradition is followed. On one hand, Islam is a religion of peace and justice. On the other hand, Islam is a religion of jihad, both a personal struggle to obey Allah and a Muslim community (*ummah*) struggle to establish the rule of Islam in the world where the straight path of Allah must be implemented and followed.

CHAPTER 4

Does Islam Allow Freedom of Religion?

Why Does Saudi Arabia Disallow Churches on Its Soil?

Why Did the Taliban Destroy Ancient Buddhist Statues?

Why Are Christians Called *Dhimmi* in Muslim Lands?

A Play on Words: Full Freedom Is to Practice Islam and Be Muslim

To understand Islam is to understand precisely how words are used. For example, peace in Islam is the peace which exists when the world of Islam is dominant over the world of heedlessness and ignorance. There is no real peace until the rule of Allah is in place. That means Islam.

Likewise, the issue of freedom of religion rests on the rule of Allah in place. The Qur'an states that there is no compulsion in religion (Qur'an 2:256). In practicality freedom of religion means that if one is not born a Muslim, it is best for one to convert to Islam. If there is not conversion, there are consequences which the Islamic community (*ummah*) brings upon those who do not submit.

The perfect religion is Islam. The Qur'an asserts that Allah has chosen Islam to be the correct religion (Qur'an 5:3). It further states that if anyone desires a religion other than Islam, it is unacceptable and in the hereafter that one will be among the lost (Qur'an 3:84–85).

When one examines the history of Islam, one observes many instances of the denial of freedom to non-Muslims and restrictions of their rights and the denial of the basic rights to Muslims who are born into Islam to leave the religion. Apostasy has serious consequences.

Conversion, Capitulation, and Conflict

When Islam has been the majority of the population and has attained political power to enact policy and legislation, often it has moved to the implementation of Islamic legal systems and jurisprudence called Sharia. Freedoms of non-Muslims have been affected, especially the freedom of religion. Non-Muslims, especially Jews and Christians, have been subjected to less than full citizenship with full rights and privileges. They have become dhimmi, a tolerated minority.

A classical pattern of Islam in the treatment of non-Muslims may be seen in the words *conversion, capitulation,* and *conflict.*

Conversion: Since Islam is the perfect religion based on the Qur'an, the Hadith, and the Sharia, all people should become Muslims from whatever their religion or nonreligion and accept Islam. Those people enjoy all the privileges that Muslims have in the society.

Capitulation: Particularly if Jews and Christians, called in the Qur'an "People of the Book," refuse the invitation to become Muslims and accept Islam and join the community (*ummah*), they may be considered as a minority people (*dhimmi*) and live under certain restrictions while remaining Jews and Christians.

Conflict: If there is not conversion or capitulation to the Islamic authority, there may be serious consequences for non-Muslims, including conflict and war.

Jews and Christians: Special Treatment

Jews and Christians, whom the Qur'an calls "People of the Book," have been given special status as minority peoples in the world of Islam. Minority status means they are given certain freedoms of worship, organization, and religious celebrations following the church or synagogue calendar. They have been allowed also to administer their own sectarian law courts on domestic matters of marriage, divorce, and inheritance.

However, Jews and Christians live under the laws of the Islamic authorities and must not conflict with them. They are required to pay taxes for their security and well-being. Often there are restrictions on any proselytism by their communities as well as locations and additions to their religious properties.

W. Montgomery Watt, noted British scholar of Islam, has written in *Muslim-Christian Encounters* concerning the treatment of minorities by Islam:

> On the whole Muslim colonist regimes behaved very fairly toward their minorities and did not oppress them. The worst that could happen was that in a time of crisis a mob could get out of hand and attack minorities, but this was rare. Apart from this, however, the members of the minorities always felt that they were second-class citizens, excluded from the Muslim elite and from many government positions. Moreover,

while a Muslim man could marry a woman from the
minorities, a man from the minorities could not marry
a Muslim woman (p. 62).
Watt concludes that Christians lived under a benign form of
Islamic colonialism.

What Happens to Apostates Who Leave Islam?

Islam is more than a religion for individual practice. It is a
religion which connects the individual to family, mosque, community, and often nation. In fact, a Muslim is a member of the
world of Islam (*ummah*). Thus, when a Muslim makes a decision to give up Islam for another religion, the decision threatens
the wider communities of which the Muslim is a part. The
family is embarrassed and loses respect. The mosque and
the community feel they have failed their duty in their relationships. And the world of Islam has lost someone to the world of
heedlessness, ignorance, and war.

The Qur'an views the apostate as one who is led by the evil
one and turns against the guidance given by Allah. The apostate
faces the wrath of Allah in leaving Islam (Qur'an 47:25–28).
Islamic law (*Sharia*), based on the Qur'an and the example of
Muhammad and tradition, has treated apostasy as an unforgiv-
able sin. The apostate is brought before the Islamic authorities
and given the chance to repent and return to Islam. If not, the
apostate forfeits life and may be punished in several ways,
including excommunication from family and community and
at times death.

Maulana Maududi has written that in the full twelve centuries of Islam before the nineteenth century, the Muslim world
was unanimous on treating apostates as infidels and blasphemers (*kufr*) and due the full punishment and wrath of Allah. As
Muslim societies tempered their legal systems with western
influences of law, the punishment for apostasy also was changed

or sometimes ignored. However, Islam's harsh treatment of apostates is alive and well across Muslim cultures.

The laws against apostasy raise the issue of Islam's view and practice of freedom of religion. Islam teaches that once a Muslim, always a Muslim. A person has freedom to leave Islam only to be declared an apostate with serious consequences and penalties. King Hassan II of Morocco, who is also the Islamic leader of his country, has said that if a Muslim chooses to leave Islam for another religion, that one will be required to have a medical exam, to seek repentance and return to Islam, and if not, will be judged.

Modern Examples of Freedom of Religion in the Muslim World

There are more than forty countries with majority Muslim populations. The four largest Muslim countries, which comprise 43 percent of the Muslims of the world, are Indonesia, India, Bangladesh, and Pakistan. These countries approach human rights and freedom of religion in a variety of ways. Because of religious conflicts in India, Muslims founded the nations of Pakistan and Bangladesh, wherein they hoped to have truer expressions of Islamic governance and society.

Two modern nations which have about 99 percent Muslim populations and represent in the Muslim world the zenith of Muslim history and values are Saudi Arabia for Sunni Islam and Iran for Shia Islam. These two countries are among the greatest Islamic peoples who engage in missions (*dawa*) around the world. They exert great influence for the causes and practice of Islam.

Denial of Freedom of Religion in Saudi Arabia

Saudi Arabia is the gatekeeper of Islam. It is the country of the birth of Muhammad and the origin of Islam. More than one billion Muslims each day face the holiest city of Islam, Mecca,

Saudi Arabia, and say their prayers in the Arabic language. Each year millions of Muslims travel to Mecca for the sacred Islamic pilgrimage (*hajj*), and some continue to the city of Medina where Islam was begun as the community (*ummah*) and where the first mosque was built and where the tomb of Muhammad is. Wahhabism, an ultraconservative form of Islam, began in Saudi Arabia in the eighteenth century and has continued to influence the government and royal family of Saudi Arabia.

Freedom of religion is near nonexistent in Saudi Arabia. No churches can be built. It is illegal to read the Bible or to conduct non-Muslim worship services. Conversion to Christianity by a Saudi citizen is punishable by beheading according to Islamic law (*Sharia*). Since the Gulf War of 1990–1991, hundreds of cases of arrests and persecution have been documented by Amnesty International of Christian foreign workers who participated in private worship services.

Saudi Arabia does not follow the classical "three-C" pattern of Islam's relationship to non-Muslims. It appears to include conversion and conflict and omit capitulation.

The Islamic Republic of Iran and Tensions in Freedom

Ayatollah Khomeini established the Islamic Republic of Iran in 1979 when the shah of Iran went into exile. Under the shah, there had been positive patterns of freedom of religion among the minorities, even though Iran was nearly 99 percent Muslim.

With the establishment of the Islamic Republic of Iran, freedom of religion was corroded, minorities were threatened in the restrictions upon their freedoms, expatriate Christian workers were asked to leave, some churches were closed, and some deaths occurred. Certain Iranian Christian clergy were murdered in the early days of the revolution, presumably because they were considered apostates, having left Islam to become

Christians much earlier in their lives. A tighter net was drawn around the native Christian communities and synagogues.

The Baha'i community received the strongest repression under the Iranian authorities. Baha'i leadership was removed from across the nation through persecution, imprisonment, and execution. There was such cruelty that a United States president and congress spoke out against it. The Baha'i were considered heretics, pagans, and a political threat to the Islamic Republic.

Iran is the premier Shia nation of Islam. It has manhandled human rights and freedom of religion. It has sent out its form of Islam throughout the world in its missionary movement (*dawa*). It declared a jihad against its neighbor Muslim nation of Iraq and a jihad against Salman Rushdie, author of *The Satanic Verses*. It is a strong supporter of Hezbollah and other militant Islamic groups.

Other Muslim Nations and Peoples

If Saudi Arabia is the guardian of the gates of Islam, and if Iran is the epitome of an example of a Shia Islamic nation in action, then many Americans are puzzled by the statements made in the name of Islam, that Islam promotes freedom of religion, and that there is no coercion in religion.

Egypt

Egypt is considered a moderate Muslim nation. It has a population of fifteen million Coptic Christians who represent one of the largest minority religious communities. Cairo is the city where the most prestigious Muslim university in the world is located—Al-Azhar. Egypt has given birth to some of the most revolutionary Islamic thinkers and writers of the twentieth century. The writings of Al-Banna and Sayyid Qutb have provided revolutionary and often militant fervor to Islamic militant groups around the world who desire to see the world of Islam established. Anwar Sadat was murdered on the reviewing stand of a military parade in Cairo in 1981 by a soldier inspired by Islamic militancy. Egyptian authorities continue to crack down on Islamic militancy.

Freedom of religion is always tenuous across Egypt. It is nearly impossible for a church to obtain a building permit to paint its walls or to make an addition to the building. Christians are often harassed by Muslims, sometimes persecuted and arrested, and sometimes killed. The charge of opposing Islam is leveled at any Egyptian Christian who may influence a Muslim to become interested in Christianity and to accept Christianity. Egypt exiled the militant Islamic cleric, Sheikh Rahman, who came to the United States and established his militant Islam at

Islamic Center in New York City

a mosque in New Jersey. He is now serving a life sentence for his leadership in the 1993 World Trade Center bombing. Often it appears that the government of Egypt is reticent and passive when Islam attacks the freedoms of non-Muslims.

Sudan

The Sudan was declared an Islamic Republic in 1983 with 70 percent Islamic population. Almost the entire indigenous northern population is Muslim. Christians, most of whom live in the south, comprise 19 percent. A primary issue has continued to be the extent of the Islamization of the Sudan, the administration of Sharia law, and whether moderate Islam or ultraconservative Islam would prevail.

The Sudan has lived in chaos of civil war, religious antagonism, refugees, and famine and drought. There have been wars between the Christian south and the Muslim north. There have been attempts to eliminate a viable Christian presence; bombings and destruction of Christian villages and churches, and the killing of Christian leaders. It is estimated that since 1983 the Muslim Arab north has killed two million non-Muslim blacks in the south. Five million have been displaced. Slavery, rape, and torture have been plentiful. Thus, when Sharia law is introduced by Islamic authorities in a society, the effect upon the freedom of religion is enormous. Christians and churches receive the impact of restrictions and often persecution and death.

From Indonesia to North America

In Indonesia, the Philippines, and India there have been tensions between militant Islamic groups and Christians. Lebanon has attempted to work out a political and social system in which both Christians and Muslims could share in common interests. The liberated republics of Central Asia, since the downfall of the Soviet Union, struggle for identity in religion and its freedoms after decades under communism.

Islamic growth in Europe and the United States has seen Muslim populations increase in numbers and mosques and economic and political influence. These Muslims living in Western societies with a history of the freedom of religion have to deal with their understanding of Islam in free and democratic societies. Most often they have more freedom of religion as immigrants than they had in their native Islamic lands. Recently Muslims in Canada have argued for the practice of Sharia law for their communities.

The challenge Islam faces in the issue of freedom of religion is most vivid when a Muslim society or group desires to combine jihad and Sharia. When Muslims are in a majority of the population and have Islamic authorities to instigate and administer this form of Islam, it presents great challenges to freedom of religion of minorities as history has demonstrated. When Muslims are an emerging and growing community with a strong minority voice in a society that promotes freedom of religion and the separation of institutionalized religion from state administration, they face the issues of how the Qur'an, the Hadith, and Islamic law traditions may or may not be a part of the political and social order.

CHAPTER 5

Does Political Islam Have Allah as Head of State?

Does an Islamic Republic Have Sharia Law as Its Rule?

In a World of Nation-States, How Does Islam Address the Issues of Theocracy, Separation of Religion and State, and Religion and Politics?

Political Life and Islam

Islam is one of the foremost religions that integrates all dimensions of life: religious, social, economic, and political. According to Kenneth Cragg, author of *Muhammad and the Christian*, to study the history and theology of Islam "is to encounter the most resolute and unperturbed of all faiths in placing trust, and finding pride, in political religion" (p. 32).

Islamic political and governmental life adheres to the principles and practices of a theocracy—that is, rule in the name of Allah. Islamic societies throughout the centuries have had various forms of government, and for the most part they have honored Islamic law to varying degrees.

Muhammad established Islam in the seventh century; his rule has been characterized as "the Constitution of Medina." Muhammad used his visions from Allah, which have been codified in the Qur'an, in ruling over the nascent Muslim community (*ummah*). He served as prophet, patriarch, judge, and commander in chief. The fundamental guideline for political Islam establishes Allah as its founder.

After Muhammad's death, a collection of his sayings and actions, known as Hadith, was assembled and has served as models for political life. Islamic traditions (*sunna*) developed under the first rulers (*caliphs*) which became a body of Islamic law (*Sharia*). The Sharia has taken different interpretations and forms by various Muslim scholars, jurists, and leaders over the centuries. Muslim nations have employed Islamic law to differing degrees.

The Ottoman Empire was ruled by caliphs who administered Islamic law. Modern Turkey, the former seat of the Ottoman Empire and still predominantly Muslim, had a secular government with the beginning of Kemal Ataturk in 1924. Presently, Islam is having a resurgence in Turkey. The constitutions of modern Saudi Arabia, Iran, Sudan, and Malaysia state that they rule under Islamic law.

Muhammad's Example of Rulership and Governance

Muhammad fled Mecca to go to Medina in AD 622 upon invitation of various leaders in Medina to establish peace and stability among the tribes. His preachments had brought threats upon his life by the tribal leaders in Mecca, his hometown.

Their polytheism, economy, and tribal relations had been threatened by the preaching of monotheism and brotherhood by Muhammad.

He implemented "the Constitution of Medina." It described the new and emerging community of believers (*ummah*) under the authority of Allah and his status as the messenger of Allah. Muhammad had authority not only as the last and seal of all prophets given to him in the Qur'an but also to be political leader, instigator, and judge of laws and punishments, and to be commander in chief of the militias he formed for security and expansion.

He decided all disputes and handed out justice in the name of Allah. He had power to give guarantees to tribes. As military chief he defended Medina and initiated raids against rebellious tribes. He claimed one-fifth of the spoils from battle. He appointed some to collect taxes. His emerging brotherhood of Islam or ummah or "nation-state" was closely allied to the Qur'anic injunctions of the worship center of the mosque, prayers, pilgrimage, and jihad.

At his death in AD 632, Muhammad had assembled the union of tribes across the Arabian peninsula into a Muslim "nation-state" with law and order and taxes and a powerful militia and religious practices under the umbrella of a monolithic Islam. Mecca also had come under the auspices of Islam and Muhammad's rulership as prophet/king. Jewish tribes had either been co-opted, converted, or annihilated. As Islam expanded, pagan tribes and peoples were to be drawn into Islam or to be conquered.

Zenith of Islamic Power and Expansion: Damascus, Baghdad, and Constantinople

Muslims look with pride to the past when their religion was at its heights in power and prestige. There are at least four epoch historical periods when Islam flourished in civilization and expansion. These were the times when religion and governance were vitally united.

The time of Muhammad's establishment of the "nation-state" in Medina (AD 622–632) was foundational and unique. After his death four rulers (the first four caliphs AD 632–661) continued the spread of Islam beyond the Arabian peninsula into the heartland of the Middle East.

Damascus became the capital of the Umayyad Caliphate from AD 661 to 750, from which Islam spread westward across North Africa into Spain and the edges of Europe. It spread eastward through Iraq, Iran, and India to the borders of China. It was a momentous expansion in a relatively short time.

Baghdad from AD 750 until about 1258 became the headquarters of the Abbasid Caliphate. For five hundred years Islam reveled in its great civilization. It excelled in mathematics and science, in art and architecture, in literature and languages. The associations of the mosques and the marketplaces, the mullahs and the rulers depicted Islam at its zenith. There were factions and schisms among Muslims during this time, but Islam provided a glue to hold the civilization together.

The Ottoman Empire ruled in Constantinople from AD 1517 until its fall under the aegis of Kemal Ataturk in 1924. Its expanse was great, its inner frictions evident, and its multiplicity of races and languages and ethnicities immense. Again Islam was the cement that undergirded the empire. Numerous conditions caused its fall, including corruption of rulers and the clergy class and the intrusions of Western economic and political and cultural institutions and values.

Thus, in reviewing their history, Muslim senses of identity and accomplishment and pride as a people and as a religion are awakened to the four primary times of Muhammad, the Umayyads, the Abbasids, and the Ottomans. These were times they remember as fact or hope in which Islam was the world of

Islam and dominated the world of ignorance and heedlessness. They believe that Islam has that possibility in the modern world.

The Modern Rise of Islamic Militancy and Revolutionary Themes

The rise of Islamic militancy has been growing since the early 1800s. The intrusion of Western influence among Islamic countries, especially in the Middle East, North Africa, and South Asia, has been viewed by Muslims as the "coming of the infidel with immorality and corruption of Islamic institutions and values." Also, they considered many of their own Muslim leaders as pawns of the West and secularizers of Islam. Thus, they felt threatened from outside by the infidel and from inside by their own apostate regimes.

Osama bin Laden awakened non-Muslims and Muslims alike to a kind of violent militancy voiced in the name of Allah and Islam that had not been seen in recent times. His militancy was influenced by the radical movement of Wahhabism begun by the reformer-revolutionary Al-Wahhab (AD 1703–1787) in Saudi Arabia. Al-Wahhab presented a radical Islam based on literal interpretations and implementations of the Qur'an and Hadith. The Saud royal family formed alliances with the Wahhabi and have ruled Saudi Arabia with this puritanical Islamic teaching.

In Egypt the Muslim Brotherhood (Al-Ikhwan Al-Muslimun) was founded in 1927 by Al-Banna with his devotee, Sayyid Qutb, continuing the movement. The movement was a reaction to British influence in Egypt and the corrupting of Islam and the secularizing of the government. The Brotherhood wanted to install Islamic rule by various means including violent jihad. Al-Banna was executed by the government. Qutb was imprisoned. President Sadat was assassinated by a soldier of the Brotherhood in 1981. And Egypt has suppressed militant Islam rigorously since World War II.

The militant teachings of Al-Banna and Qutb were spread by the Brotherhood to Jordan and Syria and to groups in India, Iran, and Iraq. The Fedayeen-e-Islami movement was begun by Muhammad Nawab-Safavi in Iran in the 1930s with slogans for his followers to take up guns rather than use prayer beads to silence the enemies of Islam.

Abul A'la Maududi formed the militant Jamaat-e-Islami in the Punjab in 1941. When Pakistan separated from India in 1947, Maududi attempted to get the government to adopt Sharia law for its governing and legal system. Thousands of Islamic schools (*madrasa*) in Pakistan teach children militant Islam with jihad as holy warfare to overcome the infidels.

With the overthrow of the shah of Iran by Ayatollah Khomeini in 1979, Sharia was established with the beginning of the Islamic Republic of Iran. America, Americans, and United States foreign policy became targets of militant Islam, inspired and supported by Iran.

Militant and revolutionary Islam has found expression in recent times in Iraq, Syria, Lebanon, Gaza and the West Bank, Indonesia, Philippines, Sudan, Afghanistan, Pakistan, India, the United States, and various movements in other lands.

Militant Islam is preached by Muslim clerics from the pulpits of the mosques, taught in Qur'anic schools to the children, voiced over mass media, institutionalized in government programs, exported in missionary movements (*dawa*) globally, and highly organized in militias, armies, and terrorist groups. Militant Islam readily admits that it finds its support in the Qur'an, the Hadith, the traditions of Muhammad and legitimate caliphs, and in Sharia law.

Themes and Methods on the Straight Path

There are consistent themes and methods of revolutionary, radical, and militant thinkers, writers, and activists to achieve their goals to the straight path of Islam. Of course, not all

Muslims think and act militantly. However, many Muslims read and hear about its themes and methods, and some Muslims are influenced sympathetically to support them through finances and morale. Other Muslims join their movements as a form of mission (*dawa*), in militias, and as suicide bombers.

Militant Islam has a *diagnosis* about the world, a *cure* for the world's problems, and a *means* to accomplish the cure.

Diagnosis: Islam has the answer for the problems of the world. The answer is found in the Qur'an, the Hadith, the traditions of Muhammad and the first caliphs, and the Sharia law systems. The problem of the world is that it is not following Islam, the established religion of Allah. The problem of the world is that it is characterized by infidels, corruption, immorality, ignorance, heedlessness, and war. Therefore, the battle is between the world of Islam and the world of the infidel.

Cure: Muslim peoples are not able to give submission to Allah and follow the straight path which the prophet Muhammad was given by the angel Gabriel from Allah in heaven. First there are ignorant and secularized Muslim rulers and leaders of Islamic peoples and societies who suppress true Islam. These leaders who are considered infidels must be removed by various means including violence and assassination. Second, imperialists and colonialists who have brought their corrupt and immoral and non-Islamic institutions and values into Islamic societies and have oppressed Muslims must be eradicated. Thus, the cure is to be found from the riddance of both the internal infidels and from the external infidels.

Methods of Achieving the Cure: True believers must be awakened to the dangers, educated, organized, and sent on a mission (*dawa*) of jihad against all corrupters and corruption of Islam. In majority Islamic nations where there are infidel government leaders, true believers must protest against them, chase them or vote them out, or use violence against the government and assassinate the leaders. In nations where

Muslims are a minority, true believers must be patient and vigilant until such time as majority status is achieved or at such time when militant violence may be used against the citizenry and its leaders to affect change to the world of Islam.

Militant Islam holds forth the plum reward to martyrs (*shahid*) who make the ultimate sacrifice in death to bring about the world of Islam. Martyrs are promised immediate great rewards from the Qur'an, from the sayings of the prophet Muhammad, and from the preachments of the Muslim clerics and the training in the militias. Hundreds of thousands of martyrs were influenced by Ayatollah Khomeini in the Iran-Iraq War. Multitudes of Palestinian suicide bombers have given their lives as martyrs against Israel. Osama bin Laden and his affiliates have led many martyrs to take the lives of thousands of non-Muslims and Muslims alike in the United States, in Yemen, in Kenya and Tanzania, in Afghanistan, in Iraq, and in Saudi Arabia.

Thus, among modern nation-states in a closely related global network of communication and interdependence, Islamic nations give various answers and expressions to the ways Islam relates to government, politics, economics, various pluralisms, and other religions. Some have monarchies with or without parliaments. Some have presidents with various forms of political assemblies. Some rely on Islamic jurists and Islamic legal systems for counsel and for shaping laws and cultural life. Some ignore the centralities of Islam. Among those nation-states and rulers where Islam is dismissed or greatly restrained, militant Islam has raised its virulent voice and has announced its greatest opposition.

CHAPTER 6

How Does Wearing a Veil Make a Woman More Muslim?

What Are the Islamic Guidelines for Gender Relationships?

Why Are Women Segregated in the Mosques?

Why Are Women of Saudi Arabia Denied a Driver's License?

What Mass Media Shows about Muslim Women

Americans see Muslim women on television and in shopping malls wearing veils. Some women are completely covered except for a screen over their face so that they may see. Some women wear head scarves, exposing their faces and wearing a covering from neck to feet. When the Taliban ruled Afghanistan, women were forbidden to work outside the home, girls were denied education, and local male committees patrolled the neighborhoods to make certain females observed the stringent codes of dress and behavior.

Saudi Arabia has multiple restrictions upon women, including no driving privileges. In Egypt and Jordan and other Islamic nations, women may or may not wear the veil in public, may receive the highest degrees of education, and may be employed in the professions. Thus, there appear to be varieties of roles for women in Islam.

- What does the Qur'an require in the roles of females and males in relationships?
- What did the prophet Muhammad say about the role of women?
- What guidance do the Islamic law courts and traditions give about women?
- How are modern Islamic societies dealing with these issues for women?

The Qur'an Says and Muhammad Recites

Veiling and Marriage

The status of women in Islam is a subject of much interest among non-Muslims. Since the Qur'an is the primary source of all authority for Islam, what it says is important. And since Muhammad is the vessel of the recitation of the Qur'an, what he said and exampled is authoritative. The Qur'an stipulates that men are to be the protectors and supervisors of women's behavior. Women are to be obedient to men. Fathers and brothers and uncles have special obligations to protect the females of the family to maintain honor and respect and to head off shame.

In marriage wives are subject to their husbands. If wives demonstrate disloyalty and ill conduct, husbands are directed first to admonish them, second not to sleep with them, and third to beat them lightly. If wives become obedient, then husbands accept them without punishment. Wives are subject to the control of their husbands (Qur'an 2:223; 4:34).

The veiling and seclusion of women have been a part of Muslim culture over the centuries. In the Qur'an, Muhammad is commanded to tell his wives and daughters, as well as the wives of true believers, to draw veils close around them. The veil would allow them to be recognized but not molested (Qur'an 33:59). He also preached that men should lower their gaze and guard their modesty in the presence of women. Likewise, women should lower their gaze and draw their veils over their bosoms so as not to display their beauty except to their husbands and their fathers (Qur'an 24:30f).

Muhammad's Wives and Polygamy: Unique for Muhammad? Examples for Others?

Before Islam a man could have as many wives as he could maintain and support. The Qur'an allowed a man to have two, three, or four wives simultaneously as long as he treated all with equity. Muhammad himself was given a special revelation with the right to an unlimited number of wives. The Qur'an stipulated that he could marry prisoners of war, daughters of uncles and aunts, and any believing woman (Qur'an 33:50).

It is estimated that he had nine to thirteen wives/concubines. His first wife was Khadija, whom he married when she was forty and he was twenty-five. After her death he married widows and divorcees. He married Aisha, the daughter of Abu Bakr, an early convert and the first caliph. Aisha was six years old at the time of engagement and nine years old when the marriage was consummated. Tradition indicates that Aisha was his favorite wife for the last nine years of his life.

Authoritative traditions (*Hadith*) indicate that Muhammad was given the strength of thirty men in his relations with his wives. He visited with each regularly in their residences. His favoritism toward young Aisha caused jealousies and problems with the other wives. The other wives sent Fatima, Muhammad's daughter, to request him to spend equal time with each wife. He responded that revelations came to him in bed with Aisha and not with the others. He asked them to love Aisha and accept things as they were.

In many Islamic nations it is rare for a man to have more than one wife. National laws have placed restrictions on multiple marriages. These prohibitions have grown out of public conscience and the impact of modern education and Western legal systems. Polygamy was abolished in Turkey in 1926, and legislation has curtailed it in Egypt, Syria, Iran, and other Muslim nations. Generally it is understood that a Muslim man may marry a non-Muslim woman while a Muslim woman may only marry a Muslim man.

Another form of marriage, known as Mut'a, developed in Islam. It is an arrangement sanctioned by the religious authorities in which a man may take a "wife" besides the one(s) he has for a temporary sexual relationship. The contract is given the man by an Islamic authority while he is away from home, for example, in military service or on a pilgrimage away from family.

Women's Rights

In pre-Islamic times female babies were slaughtered in the practice of female infanticide. Islam brought protection to females at birth. Muhammad's first wife, Khadijah, operated a business of trade sending caravans beyond the Arabian peninsula. Muhammad benefited from his wife's wealth not only working with her but having leisure time, which resulted in his excursions outside Mecca to the caves where he had his visions.

In marriage in classical Islam the bridegroom paid a sum of money (*mahr*) to the prospective bride. The husband received one-half of this dowry if there were no children and one-fourth if there were children. There was no mutual ownership of property, each retaining control over their properties. The husband was to provide for the wife's sustenance. A woman could receive a portion of her parent's inheritance, although the man could receive the portion of two females.

Baydawi, a highly respected thirteenth-century Muslim commentator, outlined the Islamic view of the male authority and superiority in the areas of mental ability, good counsel, performance of duties and of divine commands. "Hence to men have been confined prophecy, religious leadership, saintship, pilgrimage rites, the giving of evidence in law courts, the duties of the holy war, worship in the mosque on the day of assembly (Friday) etc. They also have the privilege of electing chiefs, have a larger share of inheritance and discretion in the matter of divorce."

The Braswells Eat Traditional
Iranian Meal on Floor in Iran

The prohibition or seclusion of women from praying publicly in the mosque has varied over time. To pray the formal prayers in public in the mosque is one of the most obvious demonstrations of a Muslim believer's faith. Generally, the formal prayer times at the mosque are attended by men. Women may be allowed to attend, wearing their veils, and are segregated from the men.

Traditional Islam has held that the rights and responsibilities of women are equal to those of men, but they are not necessarily identical. Women and men are created equal but not identical.

In many Muslim societies women are not socially independent. They need men to act on their behalf. They are secluded from men in education and from male visitors in the home. They must ask permission to leave the home and are often limited from work opportunities. To travel long distances a woman must be accompanied by her husband or another male family member.

Women and men appear to have varying roles in paradise. A tradition relates that at the coming judgment day women will increase in numbers and men will decrease so that fifty women will be looked after by one man. Paradise will be populated by beautiful maidens called *houris* who appear to be virgins. They are favors of Allah (Qur'an 55:54–56; 44:54). Both the Qur'an and the traditions refer to weddings in paradise. Hell is described as a place of fire, boiling fire, and full of pus. A tradition reports that Muhammad said he stood at the gates of hell and found that the majority of those entering were women.

Dr. Hammudah Abdalati, a leading Islamic scholar, has summarized the Islamic attitudes toward women:

- Women are full and equal partners with men in the procreation of humanity.
- Women are equal to men in bearing responsibilities and receiving rewards.

- Women may pursue education equal to men.
- Islam gives women equal rights to contracts and earnings.
- Women have freedom of expression as men do.
- The Qur'an reproaches the thought that women are inferior to men.
- Women receive a share of inheritance although men may receive more.
- Women have certain privileges not available to men, including exemption from prayer and fasting during menstruation periods.
- Women and men pray in separate places in the mosque. This segregation is not because of inferiority of women. Prayers necessitate bowings and prostrations, and men are not allowed to touch women during prayers. If they mixed, there could be distractions.
- The veil has been associated with Muslim women. The Muslim woman should stir the passions only of her husband. She should not expose her physical attractions before strangers. The veil is a matter of honor, dignity, purity, and chastity.

Thus, the veiling of Muslim women symbolizes more than a cloth covering their bodies. It is a way of Islamic life in which women are distinct from men. Veiling results in the seclusion, segregation, and separation of women from men and from areas of public life.

Islam indicates that it has a high view of women and the family. It promotes the sanctity and importance of marriage and the family. The Qur'an and the Sunna specify roles to husbands and wives. Generally, the husband has responsibility for the livelihood of the family, and the wife oversees the domestic affairs of the home.

The Qur'an and Islamic traditions have allowed polygamy with a man being able to have up to four wives with certain regulations. Divorce was permissible but not encouraged. Homosexuality was condemned. Abortion was strictly and basically disallowed after a specific time of fetus development.

Many modern societies in which Islam is dominant or a minority have moved more from patriarchal family arrangements to the nuclear family. Polygamy is not condoned and is frowned upon. Many women work outside the home. Therefore, Islamic forms and values of the family and gender roles have been challenged. Muslims in various cultures have different interpretations and practices on what the Qur'an and the Islamic traditions allow in these matters.

CHAPTER 7

Does Islam Have Hatred toward Jews and Christians?

Does Islam Consider Judaism and Christianity as Corrupt Religions?

Islamic Leaders Issue Commands to Kill

Americans have heard death threats against them issued by Islamic authorities with frequency since Ayatollah Khomeini's Islamic revolution in Iran in 1979. Saddam Husain and his Muslim authorities in Iraq, Osama bin Laden and his Al-Qaeda, and a multitude of Muslim clerics within Saudi Arabia and beyond have urged Muslims to strike not only against Americans but also against Christians and Jews. Sheikh Rahmam, a Muslim cleric who took up residence in the mosque in New Jersey after being exiled from Egypt for his violent rhetoric, is imprisoned for life in the United States for his conviction in the 1993 World Trade Center bombings, which resulted in deaths. Suicide bombers, namely Palestinian Muslims, kill Israeli Jews in the name of Allah.

Americans ask whether these calls, which result in violence and death for Jews and Christians and other non-Muslims, are representative of the religion Islam and the Muslim peoples in general? Is not Islam fundamentally a religion of peace and nonviolence? Do not most Muslims condemn these violent deaths by fellow Muslims? Did not President Bush say that Islam is a religion of peace, and many Muslim and non-Muslim scholars say in the mass media that Islam is not a religion of violence and destruction?

Americans are puzzled by the quietude of many Muslim leaders who remain silent about the death and violence in their religion. And they are further puzzled by statements that Americans would not be targeted unless they deserved it because of their foreign policy toward Palestine or other Muslim nations.

Muhammad's Relations with Jews and Christians

Muhammad as prophet/king and commander in chief of the first emerging Muslim nation-state related more to Jewish peoples and tribes than Christians. There were simply fewer Christians in his area. He first attempted to convert and co-opt the Jewish tribes in and around Medina into his fledgling Muslim community (*ummah*). He attempted to appease the Jews by proposing Friday as the Sabbath and establishing Jerusalem as the direction for the five formal prayers. When they refused, he selected Mecca.

He engaged in several brutal battles with the Jews. They were either expelled or executed or joined the ummah. In one last battle seven to eight hundred Jewish males were beheaded, booty collected, and their wives and children given to Muslim warriors as concubines. Muhammad later married a Jewish widow.

The classical Qur'anic teaching about the Jews and Christians is that they are "People of the Book." Muhammad basically indicates that he built upon the truths of the Torah and the Gospels (*Injil*), corrected the corruptions in the former books, and came out with the perfect Qur'an. Thus, Jews and

Christians were special people, the Dhimmi. Still they should convert to Islam. If not, they could be a minority people among Muslims, given the freedom to practice their Judaism and Christianity with restrictions, and pay the special taxes imposed upon them for this protected status. As long as they remained within these boundaries, they could be "second-class citizens."

Earlier passages in the Qur'an refer to the Jews and Christians more favorably. However, as Muhammad established Islam and required conversion and they refused to convert, his position hardened against them, and they were required to submit to the ruling authorities as "People of the Book."

Christians in the Qur'an are affirmed in following a life of prayer. They are warned not to distort the gospel. They are criticized for their obstinacy in not accepting Muhammad. They are cajoled to follow the true path of Allah which is Islam. And they are told that Allah will ultimately deal with them in the judgment day.

Muhammad established Abraham as the first true Muslim and traced the descent of the Arab Muslims through him and his son Ishmael. Moses was the presenter of the Torah to the early Jews.

Muhammad highly considered Jesus as a worthy prophet. The Qur'an gives Jesus (*Isa*) many titles of reverence including Messiah, virgin born, word of Allah, and spirit of Allah. However, it states that Jesus was no more than a messenger of Allah. The Qur'an disputes the deity of Jesus. It considers the trinity as paganism. It denies the historicity of the crucifixion in that Jesus did not actually die on a cross.

Therefore, Islam lays the groundwork for calling Christians infidels and pagans.

Islam's Affirmations of Christianity

In the Qur'an and from the preaching of Muhammad, Christianity is affirmed in the following ways:

- A religion of monotheism, prophets, angels, sacred book
- A religion of prayer, fasting, giving to the poor and needy
- A religion based on judgment day with rewards of paradise and hell
- The great prophet Jesus and his bringing the gospel

However, Islam has understood these affirmations in the context that Christianity was a pure religion in its time as preached by Jesus who was sent by Allah. After Jesus, many of the teachings found in the Bible have been corrupted by Christians. Thus, a Muslim believes that although Christians are "People of the Book" with protections given to them as minorities within the Islamic community, only the Qur'an and the teachings of prophet Muhammad give the corrected truth from the corrupted Bible.

What Has Islam Got against Christianity and Christians?

Islam is a religion that denies the major claims of Christianity. Christianity is a corrupted religion, a renegade from the true teachings of Jesus, and a colonialist and imperialist partner with the secular and crusading political powers.

The major denials and disagreements which Islam has with Christianity and Christians are:

- The present Bible of Christianity is corrupt and is inferior to the Qur'an, which is the perfect revelation from Allah.
- Christians are "People of the Book" to whom Jesus brought the truth from Allah. However, the Bible has been corrupted. Christians follow false teachings.
- Jesus is not the divine Son of God. Islam considers any teaching about the divinity of Jesus as blasphemous. Allah does not share his nature with anyone or anything. The major role of Jesus is messenger of Allah, like the other prophets.

- The teaching of the Trinity is the greatest sin (*shirk*). Muslims believe Christians are polytheists, believing in three deities, namely God, Jesus, the virgin Mary.
- Jesus was not crucified and did not die on a cross. Islam denies not only the meaning of the event but also its history. It never happened. Someone took his place.
- Jesus was not resurrected from the tomb after the crucifixion. Islam teaches that Jesus was taken up to paradise.
- Christian beliefs about Jesus being a mediator between God and humanity and the associated concepts of sin, salvation, faith, and grace are unacceptable in Islam. Islam does not believe in original sin. It basically believes that the fault of humanity is weakness and lack of correct knowledge of Allah's will and submission to it.
- Christianity's emphasis upon freedom of religion and the formal separation of religion and the political order are not Islam's teachings. Islam is the perfect religion which integrates religion with all matters of individual life and the social order. An individual born a Muslim must remain a Muslim or be declared an apostate. Freedom and peace for Islam are expressed in the context of Islam's religious and political dominance.

An Intriguing Question Americans Ask about the Muslim Jesus

One of the most intriguing questions that Americans ask is, "What are the grounds for the Muslim belief that Jesus did not die on a cross when history and historians confirm it and the Bible states it?"

Muslims are required to believe that any fact or source which is contrary to the teachings of the Qur'an is unacceptable and false. The Qur'an indicates Jesus only appeared to die on the cross. Islamic tradition states that someone took the place of Jesus on the cross.

Scholars have written that Muhammad was influenced by certain teachings of Monophysitism or Docetism, which taught that Jesus did not physically die on the cross. Since Islam does not believe that Jesus died for the sins of humanity and does not have an atonement theology of Jesus' crucifixion, his death on the cross does not have to satisfy its theology.

As far as history's validation of Jesus and his death on the cross, Islam considers the Qur'an to have precedence in historical, scientific, and social facts.

Muslim scholars assert that it is the will of Allah to permit what Allah ordains, and Allah did not permit the death of Jesus on the cross as they believe the Qur'an teaches.

A History of Conflict and Competition

The history of the relations between Christianity and Islam, for the most part, has not been one of cordiality and affirmation. Both religions are missionary to the core in their worldviews and strategies. Competition and often conflict have resulted in spreading their religions, in preaching against each other, and in warfare. The two religions have at times:

- Ignored each other out of ignorance and fear.
- Distrusted each other's motives.
- Diatribed against each other through preachments and writings.
- Fought each other in open hostilities and wars.
- Occasionally promoted friendship and understanding toward each other.

Islam's conquering armies defeated Christian lands in its spread throughout the Middle East, North Africa, and Spain in its early years. Christians became minority peoples with limitations and restrictions upon their freedoms under Islamic rulership. Residues of fear and distrust have remained.

The Christian crusades of the medieval ages to retake the Holy Land from the Muslims resulted in much bloodshed on both sides. Islam remained dominant in the Middle East centuries after the crusades. However, Christianity has been labeled a crusading religion by Islam and Christians as pagans and great infidels in partnership with the imperialistic powers that have ruled over Muslim peoples and lands.

Saint Thomas Aquinas, a seminal and influential Christian theologian of the medieval ages, wrote about Islam in his great treatise, *Summa contra Gentiles*. His writings have influenced Christian perceptions of Islam for centuries. Those perceptions have been:

- Islam is false and a deliberate perversion of truth.
- Islam is a religion that spreads by violence and the sword.
- Islam is a religion of self-indulgence.
- Muhammad is the antichrist.

Christianity and America Are Seen as Protaganists to Islam

America's rise to power in the twentieth century and its influence with the leaders of Islamic nations have been criticized by Muslim writers, thinkers, clerics, and activists. The fall of the Ottoman Empire to the secularism of Ataturk after World War I, the foreign policy of America in support of secular, nationalist, quasi-religious leaders such as Anwar Sadat of Egypt, King Husain of Jordan, the shah of Iran and others, and the unequivocal backing of the nation of Israel with American foreign policy support and finances have led Muslim Islamists, jihadists, and moderate Muslims to attack United States politics and policies.

Christian missions to Muslim lands and peoples with the purpose of evangelization and proselytism of Muslims to Christianity have been met with suspicion and resistance. Islam has aligned Christianity with American foreign policy arrogance and colonialism and Christians with the immorality and corruption and decadence of American values and culture.

Thus, when there have been efforts at fostering better relations between Christianity and Islam, often they have been met with criticism and resisted by those who continue to look at Christianity as a polytheistic religion, as a crusading religion, and at Christians as immoral in their behavior, decadent in their values, and ignorant in their beliefs.

When world cultures and nations are surveyed in contemporary times, one sees hostilities, conflicts, and war between Christians and Muslims. Violence often demonstrates hatred between the two which has festered over time from tribal, ethnic, political, and religious divisions and differences.

Examples of Conficts

Examples of hostilities and conflicts between Christians and Muslims are:

- Lebanon: Christian and Muslim militias have battled each other.
- Armenia and Azerbaijan: Religious, nationalistic conflict between Christian Armenia and Muslim Azerbaijan.
- Philippines: Muslim and Christian clashes in the islands.
- Indonesia: Muslim and Christian clashes in the islands.
- Sudan: Conflicts are deep between Muslim official government in the north and Christians in the south.
- Nigeria: Christian and Muslim tribal warfare.
- Bosnia: Old religious wounds between Christians and Muslims resulted in hostilities.
- Pakistan: Muslim and Christian tensions.
- Iran and Saudi Arabia and Afghanistan: Christians live under restrictions of Islamic governments.

CHAPTER 8

Is the Allah of Muhammad the Same as the God of Jesus?

Why Do Muslims Say the Bible Is Corrupt?

Why Does Islam Deny Jesus Actually Died on a Cross?

Do Muslims Believe Jesus Is as Important as Muhammad?

Who Are Allah and Muhammad?

Allah is one of the deities worshipped by pre-Islamic tribes in the Arabian peninsula. There were four prominent deities, namely Kuba the chief god of the Ka'bah, and three sister goddesses Al-Lat, Al-Manat, and Al-Uzza. At one time Muhammad the prophet claimed the three goddesses but later changed his mind. He said that Satan had corrupted his thinking. The verses

71

in the Qur'an that record his thinking are known as "the Satanic verses" (Qur'an 53:19–23; 22:51–53).

Another god among the tribes was Al-Illah, considered a supreme deity. Poets referred to him as Allah. *Allah* literally means "the god." Muhammad had visions in which the angel Gabriel appeared, bringing him words which later became the Qur'an. Muhammad began to preach the one true, eternal god, Allah, and no other deities were equal to him (Qur'an 112:1–4).

Thus, Allah became the god of Islam and Muhammad his prophet. Another ancient deity of the desert became important to Muhammad. It was *Al-Rahman*, which means "merciful." He used the word *Al-Rahman* (merciful) 169 times in the Qur'an to describe the nature of Allah, more than any other term.

The Qur'an required that Allah be called by his beautiful names although it does not list them (Qur'an 59:22–24). A tradition reports that Muhammad said that Allah has ninety-nine beautiful names, and to memorize and repeat them in worship will gain entry into paradise. The names are associated with the terms *life, knowledge, power, will, hearing, seeing,* and *speech.* Each chapter of the Qur'an begins with the words, "In the name of Allah, Most Gracious, Most Merciful."

Muslims use prayer beads (*tasbih*) and count off the ninety-nine beautiful names of Allah. Allah is a holy name given to Muslims through the angel Gabriel to the prophet Muhammad who is the final prophet. It is important to use the name in Arabic.

The basic relationship between Allah and Muslims is that Allah is lord (*rabb*), and humans are slaves (*abd*). There is to be total submission of the slave to the will and law of Allah. Islam teaches that Allah is one and transcendent. The great weakness or ignorance or sin in Islam is to associate the nature of Allah with creation and with humanity. Thus, Allah reveals his will to humanity but not himself. Allah cultivates no personal relationship with humans.

The Qur'an states that Allah will not forgive idolatry or the setting up of partners with Allah or believing that Allah shares his nature with anyone or anything (Qur'an 4:48). Islam directly and emphatically disagrees and opposes Christianity's teachings about the Trinity, Jesus as the Son of God, and Jesus' crucifixion on the cross. Muslims say that these Christian beliefs are pagan and blasphemous and polytheistic, for they distort the unity (*tawhid*) and transcendence of Allah.

Who Is the God of Jesus?

Jesus was a Jew who grew up in Palestine among a people who believed in the deity Jehovah who was also referred to as Yahweh. Just as the world of Muhammad some six hundred years after Jesus, the world of Jesus included beliefs among the Jews of monotheism, prophets, angels, a holy Scripture the Torah, and a judgment day with rewards.

At an early age Jesus went to the temple and the synagogue, places of worship for the Jewish people. The Bible reports that

Dome of the Rock, Al Aqsa Mosque, and Wailing Wall in Jerusalem

Jesus grew in wisdom and stature among men and with God (Luke 2:52).

Around thirty years of age, Jesus was baptized by John the Baptist, an itinerant preacher in Palestine. At the baptism the Bible states that a voice from heaven was heard to say that Jesus was God's beloved Son (Luke 3:21–22). Henceforth, many names were conferred upon Jesus by those who followed his teachings and preaching. Those included Lord, Messiah, Son of God, Son of Man, Prophet, Prince of Peace, Good Shepherd, and Alpha and Omega.

Jesus lived and taught that God was like a father. He prayed to God the Father. He told parables which included the concept of God as a father, especially in the parable of the prodigal son (Luke 14:11-13). In his death through crucifixion on a cross, Jesus prayed to God as father to forgive those who crucified him (Luke 23:34).

When Jesus was asked what was the greatest of all commandments of God, he replied that there were two. First, one should love God with all one's being. Second, one should love one's neighbor as one's self (Matt. 22:34–40). Love was a central teaching of Jesus about the nature of God.

Jesus once asked his disciples who people said that he was and who they said that he was. The response was that people thought he might be one of the prophets. A disciple's response was that he was the Messiah, the Son of God. Jesus taught that he and God the Father were one (John 10:30). He once said that having seen him was seeing the Father (John 14:9). He said that he was the way, the truth, and the life, and that no one comes to the Father except through him (John 14:6).

Christianity developed a framework of theologies and creeds that included the doctrine of God, the doctrine of the Trinity, and the doctrine of Jesus Christ. These doctrines teach that God revealed himself in a unique and special way in Jesus of Nazareth. Jesus is the Son of God sent and commissioned by God to be the Savior of the world, "Emmanuel with us." Jesus was the Word of God, the way of God, the truth of God, and the life of God for humanity. The meaning of Jesus' death on the cross and his resurrection from the grave are the atonement and forgiveness of all humanity's sin and the reconciliation of humanity to God.

Where Jesus and Muhammad Come Together and Differ about God

Muhammad established Islam during his latter years (AD 610–632), some six hundred years after Jesus. Allah of the Qur'an was one of the deities in Arabia long before Muhammad. Under Muhammad, Allah became the supreme deity. He preached that Allah had sent many prophets from Adam to Abraham to Moses to Jesus with the same message to each of their peoples. Muhammad also preached that those messages of the prophets had been corrupted over time by their followers and that he brought the corrected and true message of Allah to be established in Islam.

Therefore, whatever the Qur'an said about Allah is correct. All other purported scriptures of other prophets must agree with the Qur'an and with the preaching of Muhammad.

Jesus came out of the Old Testament background and based his preaching on the Ten Commandments, the first and second of which stated that there were no other gods beside God and that idolatry was condemned. Jesus respected and relied on the preaching of the prophets before him.

However, he brought new commandments and teachings that grew out of those before him. He preached that God not only condemned murder but anger was also under his judgment; God condemned an-eye-for-an-eye and a-tooth-for-a-tooth approach to others and said that one should not strike back; God condemned the hatred of neighbors and said that one should love and pray for one's enemies.

There are vast differences between Jesus' teachings about God and Muhammad's teachings about Allah. Christianity and Islam hold in common some general concepts about God and the way God relates to humanity and the world.

General Concepts

Some common concepts about the God of Jesus and the Allah of Muhammad are as follows:

- Monotheism: There is only one God. There is Allah of Muhammad and God of Jesus. All other claimants to deity are idols and false.
- Angels: Angels are sent as messengers from God.
- Prophets: Prophets are sent by God to various individuals and peoples with particular messages.
- Sacred books: The revelations and messages of God are contained in certain holy books.
- Creator, Sustainer, Judge: God creates, sustains, and judges humanity.
- Judgment and rewards: God holds humanity accountable.
- Worship and devotion: Humanity worships God and gives devotion through praise, prayer, stewardship of life and possessions.
- Moral and ethical life: Primary concerns of God are for high morals and ethics in family life, economic life, political life, matters of mercy and justice to the needy and poor.

Chasms of Difference between Jesus and Muhammad: The Great Divide between Christianity and Islam

The major and crucial difference, among many differences, between Christianity and Islam and between the teachings of Jesus and Muhammad is their understandings of Jesus in relationship to God. The key for understanding Allah and the concept of god in Islam is through the prophet Muhammad's preaching and the references in the Qur'an. Jesus in the Islamic tradition is only one among many of the prophets of Allah. Muhammad is the final prophet of Allah. Therefore, Muhammad's teaching about Allah and about Jesus is the perfect truth as stated in the Qur'an.

The key to understanding God and Jesus' relationship to God is in the life, teachings, crucifixion, and resurrection of Jesus as presented in the New Testament of the Bible with foundations in the Old Testament of the Bible. The New Testament presents Jesus as the Son of God, the Word (*Logos*) become flesh, and the perfect expression of God's love and will for humanity. Christianity has held that there is no need for a messiah after Jesus, for God has sent and revealed his full will and love in Jesus Christ, the Son of God.

Different Souces to God and a Different Nature of God

Different ideas and ways of thinking about the Allah of Muhammad and the God of Jesus include the following:

- Sources

  Christianity: Bible, Jesus' words, church, theologians, Christian traditions

  Islam: Qur'an, Muhammad's sayings, theologians, Islamic traditions

- The Nature of the Allah of Muhammad

  Allah reveals his will and commands, not his nature. One does not know Allah. One knows what Allah calls for in submission.

  Allah is known primarily and exactly through the Qur'an and Muhammad.

  Muhammad's relationship to Allah was to recite the Qur'an to the people.

The most frequent references to Allah in the Qur'an are: merciful (169 times); omniscient (158 times); forgiving (96 times); wise (95 times); unique (89 times); mighty (44 times); the one (21 times). There is little reference of love associated with Allah in the Qur'an.

- The Nature of the God of Jesus

  God reveals himself through prophets, angels, peoples, and in his Son, Jesus Christ.

  God is primarily the God who creates, judges, sends prophets, sends Jesus his Son on mission, forgives, gives salvation, and reconciles persons to himself.

  God is a God of agape love. This kind of love affirms, suffers with, and redeems persons. Jesus' relationship to God is one of oneness and unity, of love, and of complete submission to God's will in his death on the cross.

A Variety of Schools of Thought

Both Christianity and Islam have various schools of theology with theological nuances in describing the nature of God and Allah.

In Christianity there are various branches of Roman Catholicism, Eastern Orthodoxy, and Protestantism. However, all of them relate their doctrine of Christology to their doctrine of God. They all have a doctrine of the Trinity.

Islam has several schools of thought about its doctrine of Allah.

Sunni Islam is the most orthodox, insisting that it follows the tradition (*Sunna*) of the Qur'an and the Hadith of Muhammad. Its major emphasis is on the unity (*tawhid*) of Allah. Allah does not share his nature or attributes with anyone or anything. All religious pictures are opposed. Only the calligraphy of the Qur'an may be used in devotional practices and on the walls of mosques. The Wahhabis of Saudi Arabia represent one of the most orthodox positions in Islam.

Shiite Islam, although it relies on the Qur'an and the Hadith, is founded on the twelve imams who separated from the Sunnis. Shiites look to imams like Ali and Husain for further guidance. These imams are said to have the light (*nur*) of Allah. They are treated like mediators between Shiites and Allah with creeds to them, prayers in their names, and mosques and shrines named after them.

Sufi Islam is the mystical movement within Islam among both the Sunnis and Shiites. It emphasizes emotions, the personal attributes of Allah, personal relations with Allah, love, and heartfelt religion. Sufis believe that they find Allah through introspection and inward experiences. They are influenced by the Qur'anic references to Allah as closer than the jugular vein and as seeking the face of Allah and basking in his light (Qur'an 6:52; 50:16; 24:35).

Is the Allah of Muhammad the Same as the God of Jesus?

Muhammad has hindsight of some six hundred years after Jesus (*Isa*) to critique and criticize and, in Islam's view, to correct the mistakes of Christianity in its views of God and Jesus. He preaches that all Muslims must believe that Allah has been the same for time and eternity. Muslims believe that the same Allah gave the same message of the Qur'an to Abraham, Moses, and Jesus. Therefore, the Allah of the Qur'an and the Allah of the preaching of Muhammad is the one and only deity.

Likewise, Islam teaches that Jesus never claimed to be the Son of God or that he was crucified on the cross or that he was to be resurrected from the grave. The Qur'an does not allow Jesus to pray to God as Father.

Thus, Islam's answer to the question, Is the Allah of Muhammad the same as the God of Jesus? is yes and no. It is *yes* because the correct teaching is that Jesus was Allah's messenger as stated in the perfect Qur'an. Allah was his God. It is *no* because the God of Jesus is incorrectly presented by Christianity and its corrupt Bible. Islam teaches that Allah cannot become a human being or be incarnated. Allah shares his nature with no one.

Jesus lived and taught some six hundred years before Muhammad and the establishment of Islam. Christianity is founded upon the God of Jesus. The gospel of Jesus does not speak of or forecast the religion Islam as presented in the Qur'an or of Muhammad's being the final prophet. The nature and attributes of the God of Jesus are significantly different from those of Allah as presented in the Qur'an and through the preaching of Muhammad.

Jesus' teachings, parables, prayers, and life were founded on the God of agape love who gave commandments on love based on his nature and relationship to humanity. The issues of justice and peace and human relationships were addressed quite differently by Jesus as the Son of God and by Muhammad as the final prophet of Allah.

Thus, Christianity's answer to the question, Is the Allah of Muhammad the same as the God of Jesus? is *no*, based on the gospel of Jesus and comparisons with the Allah of the Qur'an and the life and teachings of Muhammad the prophet of Allah.

CHAPTER 9

What Is Islam Like in America, and Is It Growing?

What Do Elijah Muhammad, Wallace D. Muhammad, Malcolm X, and Louis Farrakhan Have in Common?

Can Islam and America Exist within Democracy?

Facts and Figures

Muslims entered the United States in numbers with the early slave trade. Waves of Muslim immigration have occurred especially since the turn of the twentieth century with trade and business and with students enrolling in colleges and universities. An indigenous Islamic population of note arose among African-Americans, particularly with the establishment of the Nation of Islam in the 1930s.

Research into the numbers of Muslims and mosques and Islamic institutions has occurred. However, most observers agree that the data are not exact. Some facts and figures are:

- Researchers estimate that there are from three million to seven million Muslims in the United States. The *World Almanac 2001* states that there are 5.8 million Muslims. The Council on American-Islamic Relations estimates some seven million. The average of all estimates of some twenty studies of Muslim population in the United States is 5.65 million.

- The ten states with the largest Muslim populations listed in order are: California, New York, Illinois, New Jersey, Indiana, Michigan, Virginia, Texas, Ohio, and Maryland.

- There are approximately 1,200 mosques, 400 Islamic schools and colleges, 400 associations, 200,000 Muslim businesses, and more than 200 publications.

- There are more than nine thousand Muslims on active duty in the U.S. armed services.

- Muslims outnumber Episcopalians, Lutherans, Presbyterians, the United Church of Christ, and many other Christian denominations. If figures are correct that there are six million or more Muslims in the United States, then they surpass Jews and become the second largest religious group, second to Christians.

- Muslims in America are estimated to be 42 percent African-American; 24.4 percent Asian Indian; 12.4 percent Arab; 5.2 percent African; 3.6 percent Persian; 2.4 percent Turk; 2 percent South Asian; 1.6 percent American white; and 5.6 percent other.

Thus, since World War II, Islam has grown in the United States to an estimated five million-plus adherents. There are several thousand institutions and organizations across America including mosques where Muslims primarily worship. There are Islamic primary and secondary schools, colleges, research centers, publishing outlets, and mission training schools. There are various Islamic professional associations of scholars, engineers, and medical doctors. Several Islamic groups are organized to serve as lobbyists for Islamic causes on local and national levels.

Although African-Americans represent the substantial number of Muslims in America, many Muslims have come to America from various lands, gained citizenship, married Americans, and raised their children to be Muslim.

From Elijah to Islamic Institutions and Organizations

Elijah Muhammad, Wallace D. Muhammad, Malcolm X, and Louis Farrakhan are all African-American Muslims. Elijah Muhammad served as their tutor and model as he founded the Nation of Islam in the 1930s with headquarters in Chicago. The Nation of Islam was founded on a syncretism of bits and pieces of Islam, of biblical data, of a racist ideology and platform, and of many of Elijah's personal views.

After Elijah's death in 1975, his son Wallace veered toward orthodox Islam, seeking the approval and support of the worldwide leaders of Islam. He became the titular head of the Islamic community in America, receiving much financial aid from abroad. He was invited to offer prayer in the United States Congress.

Malcolm X was a loyal lieutenant to Elijah until he recognized the impurities which Elijah taught of Islam and Elijah's own lifestyle. Malcolm made his change in moving toward orthodox Islam after he visited the Middle East and made the pilgrimage to Mecca. Upon his return he exposed Elijah's erroneous teachings of the Nation of Islam and set off on his own to form an Islamic community. He was murdered in 1965 by followers of the Nation of Islam.

Louis Farrakhan was also a loyal follower of Elijah, holding prominent positions in the Nation of Islam. Upon Elijah's death and upon Wallace's swing to orthodox Islam, Farrakhan became the head of the Nation of Islam and continued Elijah's main teachings and practices with few changes. Farrakhan has little recognition among orthodox Islamic communities both in the United States and abroad.

These noted Islamic associations in the United States that may emphasize programs in America and abroad:

The Islamic Party of North America
United Submitters International
The Federation of Islamic Associations
The Muslim World League
The Muslim Student Association
The Islamic Society of North America
The Council of the Masajid
The American Muslim Council
The American Muslim Alliance
Council on American-Islamic Relations
International Institute of Islamic Thought
Institute of Arabic and Islamic Sciences in America
(extension of University of Riyadh, Saudi Arabia)
Muslim Public Affairs Council
School for Islamic and Social Sciences
Fiqh Council of North America

What Challenges Do Muslims Face in the United States, and What Challenges Do They Present to Non-Muslims?

As with any religion, what its followers do and say in one part of the world may influence Muslims in other parts of the world, as well as non-Muslims. Islamic organizations and governments abroad contribute finances and personnel and material to Muslims and Islamic organizations in the United States.

Wallace D. Muhammad has supervised monies in a trust in the United States given by international Muslims. The government of Saudi Arabia has established grants on university campuses to establish Islamic study centers. It has supported the funding of mosques and Islamic schools and teachers and literature across the United States. Its particular form of Islam, known as Wahhabism, is stringent in its condemnation of Western views and values.

The radical Muslim cleric, Sheikh Rahman, was cast out of Egypt by the government, came to New Jersey to become the leader of a mosque, and inspired and encouraged those Muslims who bombed the World Trade Center in 1993. Many of the nineteen hijackers who killed thousands of Americans and visitors in the September 11 attacks had taken advantage of the freedoms and liberties of the United States upon their admission into the country as well as the laxness of custom and airport authorities.

Muslims and Islamic organizations in the United States give moral and material and financial support to other Muslims in need around the world. Especially, Muslims have supported the causes of Palestinians on the West Bank and in Gaza.

Muslims who are American citizens, as all citizens, are encouraged to do, give to public life, the professions, education, health, science, and the religious life of the nation. They relate to worldwide Islam by making the mandatory pilgrimage to Mecca and Medina in Saudi Arabia.

Challenges Muslims Face

Muslims face several challenges in the United States. The diversity of Islam is evident and causes misunderstandings and uncertainties among non-Muslims. There is a great contrast between the Islam of Wallace D. Muhammad and that of Louis Farrakhan. How does one view and interpret the Islam of Sheikh

Rahman as related to other Islamic preachers and teachers in mosques and associations across the United States?

As Muslims grow in numbers and Islam in presence and influence in American society, the questions of how Islam may fit into democratic society and how Islam will mix within religious and cultural pluralism are raised by Americans. Americans look at the examples of Iran, the strongest Shia Muslim nation, and of Saudi Arabia, the guardian of the holy cities of Mecca and Medina, and ask, "Are these nations representative of how Islam deals with democracy, with non-Muslims, with the freedom of religion, and with non-Islamic views and values?"

With expressions of militant Islam in other parts of the world and in the United States, Americans are asking Muslims their views on the nature and function of militant Islam and their relationships to any of its militancy.

The primary challenge of Islam in America is for American Muslims to identify what Islam is and how it is to function in a democratic and pluralistic society like the United States. An equally important challenge is for Muslims to deal with the knowledge, opinions, and stereotypes of non-Muslim Americans toward Islam as information is gained through relationships with each other, through mass media, and through the actual events among Muslims worldwide and in the United States.

CHAPTER 10

How Did Islam Advance So Rapidly after the Death of Muhammad?

What Are the Significant Dates and Happenings in Islam?

Islam arose in the Arabian Peninsula between the conflicts of two empires, namely, the Byzantine Christian Empire in the West and the Persian Zoroastrian Empire in the East. As a new movement with a fresh vision and faith and with deeply committed warriors, it thrust itself beyond the Peninsula to offer an alternative to peoples between empires and within empires.

Some peoples willingly accepted Islam and became loyal followers. Others resisted and conflict ensued and deaths occurred. Jews and Christians who did not convert to Islam were given a special status of dhimmi with privileges for their appropriate worship and religious life but with restrictions not to proselytize and the requirement to pay a tax to Islamic rulers.

Within one hundred years after the death of Muhammad in AD 632, Islam spread beyond the Arabian Peninsula to the heartland of the Middle East, including Palestine and Jerusalem, across North Africa into Spain and on the edge of France, and eastward to Iraq, Persia, and into India and parts of Central Asia.

Thus, Islam moved rapidly and established roots among millions of people in diverse locations and cultures. Hardly any other religious movement has done the same so quickly and widely.

How did Islam accomplish this feat? There is no single factor. It was by force. Some call it jihad or holy warfare. It was by the capitulation of people to join Islam either by consent or by constraint. It was because some saw Islam as a liberating and stabilizing movement which offered direction and destiny to life. Like Judaism and Christianity, Islam was a movement which basically differed with others' beliefs and practices but which offered others religious and social life within the rule of Islam under certain limitations and restrictions.

What Examples Can Be Given that Islam Is a Missionary Religion?

- Islam has an organization named dawa which trains Muslims and provides materials and sends Muslims to advance Islam among the nations.
- The four nations with the most Muslims were the focus of Islamic advance and missionary activity. With 43 percent of the world's Muslims, none of these nations is located in the Middle East where Islam originated, and none speak Arabic, the original language of Islam. These countries are Indonesia, India, Bangladesh, and Pakistan. These four nations comprise nearly half of all the 1.3 billion Muslims of the world, and all are convert nations to Islam.
- Saudi Arabia, which holds to Sunni Islam, and Iran, which holds to Shia Islam, have advanced the programs of Islam worldwide through dawa throughout Africa, Asia, Europe, and the United States. They have provided

the resources of missionary teachers and preachers and merchants and professionals, provided the building of mosques and the establishment of Islamic studies programs in schools and universities, and translated the Qur'an into the languages of non-Arabic speaking peoples.

- Europe and the United States have been the focus of Islamic dawa to the extent that Islam is a religious and cultural influence to be reckoned with in Europe and has become the second largest religion in the United States.

What Are the Significant Dates of Islam in History and in America?

AD 570–632   Muhammad, the Prophet of Islam
Born in Mecca, married Khadija in 595, visions began in 610, flight to Medina in 622 (beginning of Islamic calendar), Mecca recaptured in 629, died in arms of wife Aisha in 632

Dr. Braswell with Imam and Lay Teacher in Mosque in Raleigh, NC

632–661   Early Rulers (Caliphs)
            Abu Bakr, Omar, Uthman, Ali (These caliphs were
            close associates of Muhammad, and Ali married
            Fatima the daughter of Muhammad.) Expansion
            into Palestine, North Africa, Persia
661–750   Umayyad Caliphate
            Various Umayyad caliphs ruled over Islam with
            headquarters in Damascus
            Expansion into Spain and India and Central Asia
            Husein, son of Ali, was killed by Sunni army at
            Kerbala in present-day Iraq.
            Sunni-Shia conflict and split widened
750–1258   Abbasid Caliphate
            Various Abbasid caliphs ruled over Islam with
            headquarters in Baghdad.
            Islamic renaissance in literature, art, architecture,
            science, mathematics, medicine.
            European crusades to Palestine eleventh to thir-
            teenth centuries against Muslim lands.
            Turkish clans invaded the Abbasid-ruled lands.
1258–1517   Fragmentation of Islamic Lands
            Seljuk, Mamluk, Mongol Turkish invasions.
            Constantinople captured.
            Muslims expelled from Spain in 1492.
1517–1924   Ottoman Empire
            Ottoman Turks headquartered in Constantinople.
            Safavid Dynasty of Shahs in Persia (Iran) with Shia
            Islam.
            Napoleon invades Egypt and new entrance of West
            into Middle East.
            World War I brings end to Ottoman Empire.
            Kemal Ataturk dismantles Islam in Turkey and is
            called the Father of Modernization.
1924–   Islam's Resurgence

Present   Nationalism in Islamic countries (Notably Egypt and Syria).

Shah of Iran and modernization versus traditional Islamic challenges.

State of Israel (1948) and Islamic battles over Palestine and Jerusalem.

Oil Wealth of Islamic countries and the fueling of worldwide Islamic advance.

Ayatollah Khomeini's establishment of the Islamic Republic of Iran (1979).

His export of radical Islam and his eight-year war with Iraq (1980–1988).

Persian Gulf War (1991) pitting Muslim countries against Iraq.

Islam's influence in geopolitics, international economics, and world cultures.

Militant Muslims' attacks upon Americans and American interests and others especially led by the influence and organization of Osama bin Laden and his Al-Qaeda movement.

Islam's growth to 1.3 billion adherents and to second largest world religion.

Rise of Islamic militancy and terrorism and Osama bin Laden and his allies.

Islam In America

1717   Slaves arrive who speak Arabic, eat no pork, and believe in Allah and Muhammad.

1875   Muslim immigrants from Syria and Lebanon.

1887   Mohammed Alexander Russel Webb became the first known American convert to Islam. Encounters Islam in the Philippines where he is consul.

1919	Muslims immigrate to Michigan seeking work in the automobile industry.
	Dearborn develops into "a Muslim town."
1925	Moorish Temple of Science begins with Noble Drew Ali.
1933	W. D. Fard's Temple of Islam in Detroit.
1935	Nation of Islam with Elijah Muhammad, an African-American Baptist from Georgia, headquartered in Chicago.
1952	Federal government allows Muslim servicemen to identify their religion as Islam.
1957	Islamic Center of Washington, DC, opens.
1958	Khalifa Hamas Abdul breaks with Nation of Islam and establishes Hanafi Center.
1963	The Muslim Student Association begins.
1964	Malcolm X and Wallace D. Muhammad (son of Elijah Muhammad) are expelled from Nation of Islam. Louis Farrakhan replaces Malcolm X as national spokesman.
1965	Malcolm X murdered by Nation of Islam members.
1969	Wallace D. Muhammad reinstated in Nation of Islam by his father.
1970	Ansaru Allah founded by Isa Muhammad.
1970	Nubian Islamic Hebrews established by Muhammad Ahmed Abdullah.
1972	The Islamic Party of North America organized.
1974	Muslim World League granted nongovernmental status at United Nations.
1975	Elijah Muhammad died.
1975	Wallace D. Muhammad assumed leadership of Nation of Islam.
1977	Wallace has changed his name to Warith and changed the name of the Nation of Islam to World Community of Islam in the West as he embraces

orthodox Islam and departs the racist, non-orthodox teachings of the Nation of Islam.

1977   Louis Farrakhan breaks with Warith and reestablishes the original Nation of Islam founded by Elijah Muhammad.

1982   Islamic Society of North America founded.

1985   American Muslim Mission, the name Warith chose to replace the World Community of Islam in the West in 1980, was disbanded by Warith. He said as Muslims integrated into orthodox Islam they should be known only as Muslims.

1990   Warith D. Muhammad recognized by leading Muslim nations as titular head of Muslims in America and becomes trustee of funding by oil-rich Muslim nations for Islamic growth in America.

Dr. Braswell, Bill Hern, and Muslim Professor at King Al-Saud Mosque at Shaw University, Raleigh, NC

1992   Warith D. Muhammad invited to give invocation
            on floor of United States Senate.
1993   Muslim militants attack World Trade Center with
            deaths and destruction.
2001   Muslim militants attack the Twin Towers of New
            York City and the Pentagon and crash a plane in
            Pennsylvania, resulting in thousands of deaths and
            hundreds of millions of dollars of destruction.

            Islam has continued to grow in numbers and influ-
            ence and organizations and mosques. It has
            become the second largest religion in the United
            States with more than six million adherents.
            Muslims have formed political action groups to
            lobby politicians on local, state, and national
            levels of government. Muslims became especially
            sensitive to their status in the United States with
            the attacks on America on September 11, 2001.

CHAPTER 11

What Are the Meanings of the Words and Terms Used in the Mass Media about Islam and Muslims?

Islam originated in what is now known as Saudi Arabia. Muhammad the prophet of Islam spoke the native Arabic language. The Qur'an, which is the authoritative source and final authority of Islam, is written in Arabic. Muslims believe that Arabic is the heavenly language and the language of Allah. They pray the required five prayers each day in Arabic.

While most of the world's Muslims do not speak Arabic as their primary language, they must learn enough Arabic words to recite their prayers and to recognize certain statements in the Qur'an. Therefore, most of the Muslims and non-Muslims of the world do not know or understand the intricacies of the Arabic language. For non-Arabic speakers, there are certain words and phrases with which they must be familiar in order to understand something of Islam and Muslim beliefs and practices.

Dr. Braswell with Imam in Mosque in Washington, DC

Important Islamic Terms: A Working Vocabulary

Ali. Son-in-law of Muhammad the prophet of Islam; married Muhammad's daughter, Fatima; fourth caliph of the Sunni tradition; first imam of the Shia tradition.

Allah. Arabic name for God; means "the God"; Allah was one of many deities in the Arabian peninsula before Muhammad; "Allah Akbar" means "Greater is God"; Allah is the God of the Qur'an to whom Muslims pray.

Ayatollah. A religious leader among the Shia who is given much authority; means "the sign of Allah."

Dar al-Harb. "House of War"; the areas of the world that are still ignorant, disobedient, unsubdued, and not ruled by Islam.

Dar al-Islam. "House of Islam"; the geographical realm of the world in which Islam is in full devotional, political, and legal actuality. In Islamic constitutional law, the world is divided into Dar al-Harb (territory not under the rule of Islam) and Dar al-Islam (territory under the rule of Islam); Dar al-Harb should be brought under the rule of Islam either by submission or by warfare. Jihad is the way to accomplish it.

Dawa. "Call," "Invitation"; missionary; organization for the missionary activity of Islam.

Doa. Nonritual prayer in distinction from *salat,* which is formal prayer in Arabic.

Fatima. Daughter of the prophet Muhammad; wife of Ali the fourth caliph and first imam.

Gabriel. The angel through whom Allah revealed the Qur'an to Muhammad.

Hadith. "Tradition"; reports of the words and actions of the prophet Muhammad, constituting a body of literature second only to the Qur'an as authority for Islam.

Hajj. Pilgrimage to Mecca and its environs; one of the pillars (required practices in the Qur'an) for Muslims; must be accomplished once in a lifetime.

Hijra. Hegira; the flight or emigration of Muhammad and his followers from Mecca to Medina in AD 622; the Islamic lunar calendar begins with this date as AH 1 (After the Hegira).

Husain. Son of Ali and Fatima and grandson of Muhammad; third imam of Iranian Shia.

Id al-Fitr. The feast and celebration of ending the fasting month of Ramadan which is required of all Muslims and is one of the required pillars of Islam.

Id al-Adha. The feast that celebrates the conclusion of the pilgrimage (*hajj*) to Mecca; a lamb is sacrificed by the pilgrims in Mecca as well as Muslims worldwide.

Imam. A general term for leader of the group prayer in the mosque; also among Sunni it is the caliph; among Shia it is one of the descendants of Ali recognized by Allah as supreme ruler of the world.

Injil. "Gospel"; revelation or book given by Allah to Jesus (*Isa*); Muslims believe that since Jesus the gospel has been corrupted in its present form in the Bible.

Islam. The faith, obedience, and practice of the people who follow the teachings of the Qur'an and the tradition of the prophet Muhammad and the Islamic legal traditions (*Sharia*); the final perfect religion of Allah; "submission to Allah."

Jihad. The concept of extraordinary effort or struggle in the belief and practice of Islam by Muslims; both individual and community (*ummah*) struggle often understood as a militant defense and extension of Islam.

Kaba. "Cube"; the central sanctuary in the great house or mosque in Mecca where pilgrims on the hajj circumambulate it in rituals; worldwide Muslims face the Kaba daily in their required prayers (*salat*).

Kafir. Infidel; unbeliever.

Khadija. A wealthy widow who became the first wife of Muhamad; great encourager to her husband and among first converts to Islam.

Madrasa. Schools designated for Islamic studies; often associated with a mosque.

Masjid. "Place of prostration"; a mosque; the building in which Muslims gather and pray for religious and social occasions; its major features are the minaret, the mihrab, and the mambar.

Mecca. The first holy city of Islam located in Saudi Arabia; birthplace of Muhammad; Muslims face Mecca in their required five daily prayers; the city of the required pilgrimage (*hajj*).

Medina. The second holy city of Islam located in Saudi Arabia; Muhammad fled to Medina in AD 622; the city in which the Islamic religion and community (*ummah*) were established; place of tomb of Muhammad.

Muhammad. Prophet of Islam (AD 570–632); born in Mecca; buried in Medina.

Muslim. One who believes in, belongs to, and practices Islam; "one who submits."

Qur'an. The holy book of Islam; the revelation of Allah through the angel Gabriel to the prophet Muhammad; 114 chapters (*suras*); "recitation."

Ramadan. The ninth month of the Islamic calendar; the month (*Ramadan*) of obligatory fasting as required in the Qur'an; the time when Muhammad received revelations from Allah.

Salam. Peace; the greeting Muslims exchange.

Salat. Ritual prayer performed five times daily facing Mecca; one of required pillars of Islam from the Qur'an; may be done individually or in a group in mosque.

Shahada. Witness or confession; the first required pillar of Islam from the Qur'an; "there is no god but Allah, and Muhammad is the messenger of Allah."

Sharia. Sacred and canon law based on the Qur'an (Allah's revelation), the Hadith (sayings and deeds of Muhammad), the Ijma (consensus decision by Muslim authorities), and Qiyas (reasoning by analogy); there are six authoritative legal systems in Islam; the path of duty both ritual and general behavior for Muslims.

Shiite. "Partisan"; follower of the branch of Islam that accepts Ali as the legitimate successor to Muhammad and as the first imam; believe the descendants of Muhammad should rule the Islamic community (*ummah*); Iran is the primary Shia Islamic state.

Mosque on the Campus of the University of Tehran, Iran

Sufi. A Muslim mystic; Sufism is Islamic mysticism; It seeks direct experience with Allah; it has leaders called sheikhs and communities called brotherhoods.

Sunna. The path of tradition or orthodoxy followed by Muslims.

Sunni. Term which means "those who follow tradition or reliance on the Qur'an and the Hadith and the Sharia without the unorthodoxy of the Shia"; the Sunni approved by consensus the leader to follow Muhammad at his death rather than the Shia idea of family succession.

Ulama. Scholars of Islamic theology and law; singular is Alim.

Ummah. The community of Islam; the solidarity of faith, prayer, and belief; the political incorporation of the Islamic religion; Dar al-Islam.

Zakat. Almsgiving; one of the required pillars of Islam.

CHAPTER 12

What Have I Learned about Islam from My Study and Experiences?

Audiences from civic clubs to university campuses to church groups have asked what I have learned from my experiences of living in Iran, teaching Muslim clerics, visiting in mosques and homes, doing research, and visiting and conversing and studying mosques and Muslim peoples in the Middle East, Africa, Asia, Europe, and the United States.

Teaching Muslim Preachers: Lessons Learned about Islam

Surprises! Surprises!

During the years 1968–1974, the Faculty of Islamic Theology of the University of Teheran granted me a work permit and a professorship to teach comparative religions to its six hundred students studying for master's and doctorate degrees. The faculty was comprised of learned and respected Muslim jurists and preachers. The students wore the turban and robe and graduated to be imams of mosques, chaplains in the Iranian armed services, and teachers of Islam in the school and college systems.

During my last year of teaching, the shah of Iran counseled the dean of the Faculty of Islamic Theology to admit three

females. All three sat in my class. They were above-average students. However, the males discriminated against them, made
them sit in the back of the class, and generally ignored them.
The dean made my class the pilot program to introduce women
into the school. For the years of my professorship, I was the only
non-Iranian and non-Muslim on the faculty.

I was invited into the homes of my Muslim preachers for
many meals and for celebrations of the ending of Ramadan and
other festive occasions. I was invited to meetings in many
mosques to have the honored seat next to the pulpit to hear
sermons preached without notes by famous members of the
ulama (class of preachers and jurists) to crowds sometimes
numbering over three thousand male worshippers. Women sat
in segregated quarters.

In many mosques I engaged the Muslim preacher and his
students in conversations about Christianity and Islam and
about the place of Jesus (*Isa*) in both religious communities. My
wife and I had high-ranking Muslim preachers with their board
of trustees in our home for refreshments and conversations.
They took this occasion to castigate Zionism and American foreign policy in support of Israel as well as to question how
Christians can believe that Jesus is the son of God.

Serious Hospitality: Serious Encounters

Muslims are among the most hospitable people upon the
face of the globe. Once you have established a relationship with
them, there are invitations to meals, weddings, and religious
meetings and festivities. My sons were four and five years old
upon arrival in Teheran. They learned to play soccer with
Iranian kids on the dirt streets with rocks as goals. Families of
the kids invited us for tea, and friendships blossomed around
cups of tea and tables of food. Middle-class Iranians fumed over
the slowness of the shah's reforms in good-paying jobs and
opportunities for education of the youth.

I often ate in Muslim preachers' homes sitting on exquisite Persian carpets eating rice and meat with our fingers while the women in their veils (*chadors*) served us. As a Christian and an American, I was always accepted in homes and mosques. Hospitality was genuine. I have found that hospitality among Muslim peoples the world over. But there was always an edge to conversations by the preachers about the faults of Christianity and the bad foreign policy of the United States and the immorality and corruption in the American culture. They insisted that Islam was the perfect religion with all the answers for personal life and for society.

Religious Devotion and Pride in Islam

Religious devotion was taken seriously by Muslims. Although many Muslim youth were interested in Western thoughts and some Western ways of music and clothing, they respected the Islam of their parents and the leadership of mosques, and they themselves prayed, fasted, and observed the customs of their religion. All Muslims looked to the day when they could make the pilgrimage (*hajj*) to Mecca in Saudi Arabia.

I always observed Muslim pride in their religion. From older adults to youth, they were proud of Islam, its purity and perfection for life's matters. They constantly recalled the great Islamic civilizations of the early years after the death of their prophet, Muhammad, and the high medieval ages when they ruled vast lands and the Ottoman Empire. They lamented the more recent downfall of Islam in its status as a pervasive civilization and an overwhelming political power. Usually they did not hold themselves responsible for the fall of Islam. The fault rested in outside powers and influences which they labeled as colonialists and imperialists. Some held their own leaders as the culprits for selling out Islam to secularization and westernization. They seemed always to be victims of outsiders or others' policies toward them.

Bride and Groom Wed, Led by Muslim Cleric in Iran

I met hundreds of Iranians who studied in American universities and returned to Iran to get jobs through nepotism or not to get jobs because they were overeducated and trained. As much as they wanted the technical goodies and some of the good life of America, they returned home to live with mother and father, to await the planned marriage, and to practice the devotions of Islam. At the time of the revolution of Ayatollah Khomeini and the downfall of the shah, they were pleased to see change and to taste some freedom from a secular and American co-opted shah. They shouted Allah Akbaer, "God is Great."

I learned that a Muslim worth his or her salt will pray the required prayers daily and routinely, will fast one month a year, will give to spread the religion, will recite the confession that there is only one God, Allah, and Muhammad is the final prophet/messenger, and will plan once during a lifetime to take the pilgrimage to Mecca.

One of my Muslim preacher boys epitomized the feelings and thoughts of most Muslims I met when he said to me, "You can become a Muslim. Islam is the greatest religion in the world."

Not All What It Seemed: Underneath the Obvious

Besides great hospitality to strangers and guests, and besides great respect and reverence to Islam and devotion to it, a third lesson I learned is that Muslims may practice an art form called dissimulation. They may use code words and establish relationships and act on one set of principles in order to gain and experience a later objective and goal.

Many of my Muslim preachers used code words in their preaching in the mosques to send signals to the people that Allah and the true religion of Islam would topple the shah. They feared the shah's long arm of repression. The Iranian revolution occurred in part from this kind of preaching and rallying of the forces in hundreds of mosques across the country and in secret prayer meetings in early mornings in homes and mosques to which I was invited.

Many Iranians returned home from study in America to court an American's friendship in order to gain recommendations for relatives to attend colleges in the United States. When I was one-on-one with them, there was praise for America. When I visited their extended families in homes, they would stimulate the conversation with just enough faults of America that the other males of the household would castigate

American foreign policy and the wayward ways of Americans in immorality in sex and the treatment of women and in corruption in the marketplace. They would voice that Islam and the Qur'an and the prophet Muhammad were superior in all teachings and applications in life.

Immediately after the Iranian revolution, several Christian pastors of Iranian evangelical and Anglican churches, some of whom were my friends who had converted to become Christians years before, were murdered in their homes or in the streets. For years they had been treated in dissimulation behavior. When Iran became the Islamic Republic of Iran, they were considered as apostates and murdered. A story remains to be told of the Christian martyrs of Iran.

America and Its Policies: Bad! Bad! Bad! Myself (Americans): Good! Good! Good!

After living in Iran from 1968 and into 1974, I observed many features of Islam in its heartland. In the hundreds of visits I made to the mosques and in the homes of Muslims, I was always treated with great respect and with much cordiality. I liked to think it was for who I was: an individual, a Christian, an American, and a professor at the Faculty of Islamic Theology of the University of Teheran. Perhaps it was a mixture of all of these characteristics. Individual Americans were respected and often loved. But American foreign policy and policymakers were looked upon with suspicion and condemnation. And Christianity was acceptable in polite conversations but detestable in its erroneous teachings.

One could always bank on one constant. American foreign policy and power toward Iran was always problematic with those I knew. Zionism was always detested. And often Muslims made a close connection between corruption and immorality in America with their assumption that America was a Christian nation and, therefore, Christianity was the culprit. I never met a

Muslim preacher or Muslim who practiced the essentials of Islam who did not think that Christianity had corrupted the teachings of Jesus (*Isa*), whom they accepted as one of their prophets, and that Islam was the perfect religion to take the place of all religions of the world.

Impacts upon My Understanding of Islam Today

In the last twenty years, I have visited mosques and talked with Muslims across South Africa, Kenya, Central Asia, the Middle East, Europe, and America. In the last twenty years I have taken several thousand seminarians and church folk into mosques to hold conversations with Muslim leaders. As usual, I have been befriended by them, both Muslim preachers and worshippers. I have continued to research Islam in its history, its Qur'an, its Hadith, and its contemporary settings. Although I studied Islam intimately in Iran, I learned lessons that I believe are applicable today.

Muslims are friendly, hospitable people. I, personally, have been well received by them in all cultures and various settings. I have Muslim friends today.

Muslims come in varieties of faith and practice. Certain characteristics of Muslims tend to group them into certain worldviews and behavior forms. One needs to be careful not to stereotype. Having said that, we do look at human populations with certain characteristics knowing that all do not fit the type. The best way to know and understand a Muslim is to establish a relationship and engage in many meaningful conversations.

Orthodox Muslims: Most Muslims I have met who faithfully attend the local mosques, listen to the Friday sermons of their preacher, say their five daily prayers, fast the month of Ramadan with no excuses, give their monies for the spread of Islam globally, and plan through saving their money to take the pilgrimage to Mecca, Saudi Arabia, are orthodox in thinking and practice. They believe that Islam is the perfect religion for all matters of life. They believe that the world is divided rather neatly into the world where Islam must dominate and follow Allah and into the other world where Islam is not present or is held hostage by some non-Muslim or secularist and evil Muslim ruler who has sold Islam out to the colonialists or imperialists and for their own gains. These Muslims see Islam as coming around to rule the world based on the Qur'an and the traditions and examples of their prophet Muhammad. Enemies seen are Zionism, a corrupt Christianity in morals (treatment of women) and beliefs (Jesus is God), and colonialist and imperialist nations lording over Muslim nations and peoples.

Semiorthodox Muslims: These Muslims often pick and choose among the major practices of Islam which they will observe. They may or may not frequent the mosque, and usually they do not give much time to the counsel and preaching of Muslim clergy types. Often their family members, especially the males, are practitioners of orthodoxy, and these members reprimand their relatives for not being more Muslim. The semiorthodox become offended if Islam and their prophet are attacked or belittled and join in spirit the outcries against the infidels. They do not know the intricacies of Islam but rally to the opinion that Islam is better suited to lead the world.

Cultured Muslims: Cultured Muslims are born into Muslim families. They have observed their relatives practice the rituals of Islam, but they themselves have chosen not to be a regularly practicing Muslim. They are open to other religious and philosophical and cultural views and values. Often, when the chips are down, they support Islam because it is a family, community, or national thing to do. These Muslims dwell on the notion that Islam is a religion of peace without going into the intricacies of the Qur'an, the life of Muhammad and his example, and the law and traditions of historical Islam.

Fanatical Muslims: Fanatical Muslims may or may not know and observe the intricacies of Islam. However, they do believe that Islam is the perfect religion for the world. They do believe that Islam is under attack from its enemies, namely, its sacrilegious Muslim leaders of nations who have been co-opted by outsiders, by the colonialist and imperialist nations such as America, and by the corruption of those who follow Judaism and Christianity. They basically live in a world of we versus they, belief versus unbelief, and Islam versus ignorance, corruption, and immorality. Fanatical Muslims are prone to follow a charismatic Muslim leader or clergy type, to have a plan against the enemy, and to face martyrdom in the name of Islam.

Westernized Muslims of the Intelligentsia: These Muslims have been deeply influenced by Western thought, culture, and values. They subscribe to high and elevated concepts of Islam that it is a religion of peace, freedom, and great intellectual ideas which are highly adaptable to modern societies. They voice that Muhammad was a noble, kind, and benevolent man whose characteristics are worthy of emulation. Many of these Muslims do not frequent the mosque or follow the counsel and direction of Muslim clergy.

Contemporary Islam

Contemporary Islam lives in a world where it has become the second largest religion with some one billion and three hundred million followers and is the fastest-growing religion. The heartland of Islam is the Middle East, where it was born and where its native and sacred language is spoken. Saudi Arabia presides over its two holiest cities: Mecca, where Muhammad was born and where all Muslims must face to pray five times each day and where they must make their pilgrimage; and Medina, where Muhammad is buried. Jerusalem is holy because it contains the Dome of the Rock and Al-Aqsa Mosque.

However, the four most-populous Muslim countries are outside the Middle East. They are the nations of Indonesia, India,

Bangladesh, and Pakistan. These four nations contain 43 percent of all Muslims.

Having stated these facts, one finds a rather constant pattern among many Muslims in various cultures with regard to the following:

- Islam with its foundations in the Qur'an and the traditions and examples of its prophet Muhammad is the religion which has the perfect answers for the systematic organization of a society, including its religion, political order, economics, law, and family life.
- When Islam is under attack by outside forces, it has a right to defend itself and go on the attack under the proper declarations by its clergy.
- Islam is a religion of peace when it is the dominant religion and engages its people in Islamic understandings and practices. Minorities within its borders, especially Jews and Christians, must be subservient to its rulership with certain privileges of worship and sectarian customs.
- Islam is a religion of warfare by both military action and missionary zeal in its counteraction to corruption, immorality, and ignorance. It practices jihad in both the individual life and the life of the community.
- When a Muslim chooses to leave Islam for another religion, he or she faces a crisis with family and the Muslim community which often results in ostracism and sometimes death. A Muslim male who marries a non-Muslim woman must raise the children as Muslims. A Muslim female must marry a Muslim male.

What to Make of All These Things

Arguments are made today that there is a clash of civilizations, namely, between the Western world founded upon Judaic-Christian values and that of Islamic religion and culture. Samuel

Huntington's "Clash of Civilizations" ideas have impacted the discussion of Islam's presence in the twenty-first century.

Arguments are made today that Islam is out to win the world and to rule the world in the name of Islam.

There are sentiments today among non-Muslims that Islam is a religion of violence and hatred.

Non-Muslims are raising questions today if Islam can live in a pluralistic world of global peace, freedom of religion, religious liberty, and the formal separation of religion and the political order.

Some write of the different brands of Islam in the world today, namely, fundamentalist Islam, militant Islam, jihadist Islam, moderate Islam, political Islam, and Islamists.

Some non-Muslims believe that Islam operates on the basis of the three C words: *conversion, capitulation,* and *conflict.* The primary goal in Islam is to convert all people to Islam. If people do not convert, especially Jews and Christians who are

Iranian Bride Made Sweet with
Outpouring of Sugar

Muslim Cleric Counsels
Groom in Iran

referred to in the Qur'an as "People of the Book," then those people must capitulate to Islamic rulership but are provided certain minority status privileges of their sectarian worship and traditional family law and customs. If there is no conversion and capitulation, then there may be conflict and warfare until Islam is successful.

I believe some Muslims are struggling with their roots of the past in a religion originating in a tribal and patriarchal society and their potentialities of the future in a highly modern, mobile, and technological world. However, most Muslims of the world cannot read their scripture, the Qur'an, in the Arabic language in which it was given to the prophet Muhammad. Often they rely on the preachings and teachings and interpretations of Muslim preachers, jurists, scholars, and revolutionaries. Muslim home folk and Muslim street people may be led to follow charismatic leaders in a militant jihad.

Revisiting Key Questions by Americans about Islam

Some of the questions of non-Muslims about Islam apply to the meanings and ways that Islam and the Qur'an and the prophet Muhammad and Islamic law define the following:

Peace: Is real peace for Islam when it is dominant and has political and religious power over others? Is *peace* a code word for submission to Islam? *Islam* means "submission or obedience." In practice it means submission to the Qur'an, the example of Muhammad, and the laws and traditions based on the Qur'an and Muhammad's sayings and deeds.

Jihad: Is jihad a combination of individual and community struggle to bring Islam to dominance in the world either through conversion to Islam, or submission to the authorities of Islam, or to conflict which results in either submission or capitulation or death?

Freedom of religion: Is there real freedom for an individual to remain a Muslim once born into the Muslim family or community or to leave Islam to become a follower of another religion or no religion. If there is freedom of religion, why is apostasy such an issue with Muslims> Why does it result in conflict, excommunication, and sometimes in the death of the one who leaves Islam?

Religion and politics: Is there inherent in Islam the idea of a political religion in which there is little or no differentiation between religion and the political order or system of government?

Islam is a powerful and strong religious force which dominates the heads of Muslims with a promised paradise on earth, as well as in the heavens and which dominates the bodies of Muslims with a lifestyle of praying, fasting, pilgrimage, confessing, sermon listening, and strict gender roles according to an hourly, daily, monthly, and yearly calendar. It is a religion uncompromising in its beliefs and practices, contending that it has the perfect answers for all of life's questions and pursuits and that it should spread Islam until all peoples are under its rulership and domain.

Non-Muslims look to see what kind of Islam is in Saudi Arabia, Iran, the Sudan, and other Islamic republics. Non-Muslims look to see what is now emerging in Lebanon in Islamic political expressions. Non-Muslims look to see what challenges secular Muslim rulers have in keeping suppressed political Islam in their populations in Egypt, Pakistan, Indonesia, and Algeria, as well as other nations. Non-Muslims look to see what is emerging in Europe and the United States in Islam as expressions of political Islam in democratic societies.

V. S. Naipaul, recent Nobel Prize winner, and author of *Beyond Belief*, wrote, "Islam is not simply a matter of conscience or private belief. It makes imperial demands." He made this statement after studying Qur'anic and classical Islam and studying the cultures where Islam is dominant around the world.

Kenneth Cragg, noted Anglican bishop, missiologist, and author, wrote in his book *The Arab Christian*, about a future with Islam. He described Islam as having an inherently political nature, of its abiding instinct to conscious superiority and dominance, of its "incorrigible assertion and relations of inequality, sometimes hostile and rarely other than superior," and Islam's belief that it is "commissioned with a mandate of power to institutionalize divine sovereignty on earth via the Sharia, the ummah, and the dawa (sacred law, community, and state)." Cragg, who spent much of his life living in the Middle East, was one of the few Christian churchmen to be invited to lecture at the University of Teheran while I lived in the city.

CHAPTER 13

What Change Did Muhammad Bring to the Tribes of Arabia?

What Did Muhammad Have to Do with Mecca and Medina?

Muhammad's Vision and Straight Path: From Tribalism to Islam

Muhammad was born into an influential tribe in Mecca. However, with his new religious consciousness and teachings, he became a revolutionary figure in his preaching for change from the ancient tribal customs. The tribal leaders harassed him and threatened his life. He fled for his life with his few followers to the city of Medina. In Medina he established Islam and brought cohesion to his fledgling Muslim followers. Tribes around Medina were brought into alliance with Muhammad's emerging community (*ummah*) or nation-state. By the end of his life, he had conquered Mecca and its surrounding tribes and inaugurated Islam as the superior religion. In many ways Islam became the new tribe with its unity of belief and practice.

Tribalism

The Arabian peninsula of Muhammad's time (AD 570–632) was populated by various tribes. Muhammad was born into the Quraish tribe, one of the most powerful. The tribes were characterized by competition, warfare, treaties, booty in victory, blood revenge, safe places, and seasons from retribution.

Islam's Answer: Muhammad established the ummah, the brotherhood of Muslims. The ummah became the tribe of Muslims, erasing the old tribal loyalties and alliances and uniting around Allah and the Qur'an and the Hadith. The ummah retained some tribal practices such as booty in Muslim raids and safe places and seasons such as the mosque and fasting season (Ramadan).

Patriarchy

Tribalism was characterized by male leadership and dominance. Favoritism was given to sons. Females at birth were often killed. There was a plurality of marriages and harems.

Islam's Answer: Female infanticide was not condoned. Females were granted more privileges including more rights in inheritance laws. The Qur'an limited marriages to the maximum of four if a husband could treat the wives equally. An exception to have more than four wives was granted to Muhammad.

Polytheism

The Arabian tribes worshipped and venerated a variety of male and female deities, including Allah, at a central shrine in Mecca. Animism was also a practice of the tribes.

Islam's Answer: Muhammad proclaimed monotheism (*tawhid*-unity) in the one deity, Allah, and cleansed the central shrine of all deities, and established that shrine (the Ka'bah) as the focus in prayer and pilgrimage of all Muslims. Muhammad preached that Allah does not share his nature with anyone or anything and thus attacked Christianity's teachings on Jesus as the Son of God and the Trinity and thus stated that the greatest sin (*shirk*) was to attribute God's nature to anyone.

Animism

Tribalism was characterized by beliefs and veneration of spirits, both animate and inanimate, including the moon, stars, and wind. Shrines and rituals related to these objects.

Islam's Answer: The Qur'an denied the worship and veneration of spirits and the inanimate world. The Qur'an established a category of spirit/angel types, including jinn. The Qur'an referred to Jesus as the spirit of Allah, as well as many other references.

Algerian Chief Reading the Qur'an

Legislation and Law and the Straight Path

Tribalism existed on informal rules and traditions understood by all tribes, administered by patriarchs and sheikhs, and included raids and booty, blood revenge, alliances, sanctioned times and places to exclude warfare, murder, and pillage.

Islam's Answer: Islam's straight path is founded upon beliefs, rules, laws, practices from the primary authorities in the Qur'an, the Hadith, the Sunna, and the Sharia. Islam is under the rule of Allah and his final prophet Muhammad, who serves as the excellent example for emulation by Muslims. Prescriptions are given in the Qur'an for beliefs in Allah, angels, prophets, holy scriptures, and final judgment for paradise and hell, as well as for the confession (*shahada*), giving (*zakat*), prayer (*salat*), fasting (*Ramadan*), and pilgrimage (*hajj*). Directions are also given in the Qur'an for matters of life such as family, hygiene, jihad, and martyrdom.

Islam's Tale of Two Cities: Mecca and Medina

Mecca and Medina, located in present-day Saudi Arabia, are the two holiest cities of Islam. Saudi Arabia considers itself the supreme guardian over the two cities. No non-Muslim is allowed to enter Mecca, and during certain high ceremonies following the Islamic calendar, several million Muslims from around the globe may congregate in both cities.

Mecca is the birthplace of the Islamic prophet Muhammad. It was a crossroads for traders traveling from the edges of the Mediterranean Sea on their way to India and beyond.

In a cave outside Mecca, Muhammad experienced the visions upon which Islam is founded. In the city he preached the substance of his visions to his tribal kin and others. Since he attacked the polytheistic and animistic religion practiced in the Ka'bah, a central monument in Mecca, his life was threatened. Muhammad fled from Mecca to Medina with his few followers in AD 622. That hasty departure from Mecca is known as the

Hegira, the flight from Mecca to Medina, and is the beginning of the Islamic calendar or the year 1 AH (after the Hegira).

For the 1.3 billion Muslims, Mecca is the direction to which they turn five times daily to say their prayers. It also is the city to which every faithful Muslim goes on the required pilgrimage (*hajj*) once in a lifetime, although many Muslims with finances may go many times. Islamic tradition also associates Mecca with Abraham and his son Ishmael, and the building of the Ka'bah originally around a monotheistic faith.

The city of Medina, some two hundred miles north of Mecca, is where Muhammad began to build the foundations for Islam. He was not only the prophet of the fledgling religion but also played the roles of judge, patriarch, and commander in chief of the militia. He built the first mosque there. His militia conquered the surrounding tribes. In Medina he established the Islamic community (*ummah*) or nation built on the principles in the Qur'an and his words and deeds (*Hadith*).

Washing for Prayers at Mosque in Iran

Before Muhammad died in AD 632, he had conquered Mecca, his birthplace, and established the religion of Islam with its belief in one deity, Allah; the Qur'an as the perfect scripture; and his life and teachings as the premier example for all Muslims to follow. The Ka'bah was cleansed of idols and established as the center for true monotheistic belief and practice.

He died in Medina in the arms of his youngest and most beloved wife, Aisha, and was buried in the precincts of the mosque. By this time he had become the ruler of much of the Arabian peninsula and had poised his nation on the verge of ruling over many lands.

When Muslims go on the mandatory pilgrimage to Mecca, many continue to Medina to visit Muhammad's grave and the first mosque. Some Islamic traditions encourage Muslims to gain extra merit by going to Medina to show respect for the life of Muhammad.

Thus, Mecca and Medina are always on the minds and hearts of worldwide Muslims. They are sacred cities. Not too far away is the city of Jerusalem in Palestine. Jerusalem is the third most sacred city in Islam. It is the place where Muhammad was transported from Mecca to what is now the Dome of the Rock and from which he ascended into heaven to receive further revelations.

APPENDIX 1

What Many Americans Read in Print Media, Hear on Radio, and See on Television about Islam

"The face of terror is not the true faith of Islam. That's not what Islam is all about. Islam is peace. These terrorists don't represent peace. They represent evil and war.

"When we think of Islam, we think of a faith that brings comfort to a billion people around the world. Billions of people find comfort and solace and peace. And that's made brothers and sisters out of every race.

"America counts millions of Muslims among our citizens, and Muslims make an incredibly valuable contribution to our country. Muslims are doctors, lawyers, law professors, members of the military, entrepreneurs, shopkeepers, moms and dads. And they need to be treated with respect. In our anger and emotion, our fellow Americans must treat one another with respect."

—President George W. Bush, September 17, 2001, http://www.whitehouse.gov/news/releases/2001/09/20010917-11.html.

D o m e   o f   t h e   R o c k   a n d   A l - A q s a
M o s q u e   i n   J e r u s a l e m

"The ruling to kill the Americans and their allies—civilians and military—is an individual duty for every Muslim who can do it in any country in which it is possible to do it."

—Osama bin Laden and other Muslim extremists from Bangladesh, Egypt, and Pakistan signed this fatwa [Command for Muslims to follow] "Urging Jihad Against Americans" in February 1998 with the overall title "Declaration of War by the World" Islamic Front.

"Every Muslim who sees discrimination begins to hate the Americans, the Jews, and Christians. This is part of our religion and faith. Since I became aware of things around me, I have been in a war, enmity, hatred against the Americans."

—Osama bin Laden, 1999 (interview with Jamal Isma'il) http://usconservatives.about.com/library/weekly/aa093001a.htm.

"For Islam and those who follow him (Osama bin Laden), this is a religious war, a war for Islam and against infidels, and therefore, inevitably, against the United States, the greatest power˘ in the world of the infidels."
—Bernard Lewis, noted historian of the Middle East, in *The New Yorker,* 19 November 2001)

"A writer points out that the Dome of the Rock, one of the earliest Muslim religious structures built outside Saudi Arabia about AD 691, includes a number of anti-Christian polemics: 'Praise be to God who begets no son, and has no partner.'"

"Osama bin Laden and his Al-Qaeda followers may not represent Islam, and their statements and actions directly contradict basic Islamic principles and teachings, but they do arise from within Muslim civilization, just as Hitler and the Nazis arose from within Christian civilization, so they must be seen in their own cultural, religious, and historical context."
—Bernard Lewis, noted historian of the Middle East, in *The New Yorker,* 18 November 2001.

"If a Muslim says, 'I have embraced another religion instead of Islam,' before he is called to repentance, he will be brought before a group of medical specialists, so they can examine him to see if he is still in his right mind. After he has then been called to repentance, but decides to hold fast to the testimony of another religion not coming from Allah—that is, not Islam, he will be judged."
—King Hassan II of Morocco, also the imam of his country, quoted in the daily newspaper *Al Alam* before a human rights commission, 15 May 1990.

"If this isn't about Islam, why the worldwide Muslim demonstrations in support of Osama bin Laden and Al-Qaeda? Why did those ten thousand men armed with swords and axes mass on the Pakistan-Afghanistan frontier, answering some mullah's call to jihad? Why are the war's first British casualties three Muslim men who died fighting on the Taliban side? . . . [Islamists have] a loathing of modern society in general, riddled as it is with music, godlessness, and sex; and a more particularized loathing (and fear) of the prospect that their own immediate surroundings could be taken over— 'Westoxicated'—by the liberal Western-style way of life."

—Salman Rushdie, author of *The Satanic Verses,* in *The New York Times,* Fall 2001.

"North America is the New Spain, the Golden Age of Islam."

"We have to transform the United States into Medina."

"Freedom in Islam is to do the right thing, to implement Islam."

"Other religions than Islam are only progressive ignorance."

"Non-Muslims are *kafir* (unclean, infidels)."

—Statements made by a variety of Muslim speakers at a national conference in the United States in the mid-1990s.

"Praise is to Allah who has ordained Al-Jihad (the holy fighting for Allah's cause):

1. With the heart (intentions or feelings)

2. With the hand (weapons, etc.)

3. With the tongue (speeches, etc., in the cause of Allah)

"Allah has rewarded the one who performs it with lofty dwellings in the Gardens (of Paradise). . . . I testify that there is none who has the right to be worshipped but Allah alone, and He has no partners [with Him]. I also testify that Muhammad is His Slave and His messenger, the one sent by Allah as a mercy for the Alamin [mankind Jinn]; the one commanded by Allah to fight against the Mushrikun [polytheists, pagans, idolaters, and disbelievers in the Oneness of Allah and in his Messenger Muhammad]."

—Written by Sheikh Abdullah bin Muhammad bin Humaid, the chief justice of Saudi Arabia as an attachment named "The Call to Jihad in the Quran" in The Holy Qur'an.

"Why Do They [Muslims] Hate Us?
- Sometimes it is pure jealousy and envy.
- They are envious of our prosperity and freedom.
- They often perceive us as bloated with wealth.
- Sometimes they perceive us to be an immoral nation exporting our immorality.
- Sometimes it is because of the mind-set of the fundamentalist fringe of radical Islam who think of us as their chief rival for the hearts/souls of men.
- Sometimes it is because of their perception that we are unaware and don't care about our uncritical support of Israel."

—David and Maxine King, who lived through twelve years of the Lebanese civil war and after twenty-nine years living in the area and after the events of September answered their own question.

"Muslims and all Arabs must unite to defeat the anti-Muslim Jews. The Europeans killed 6 million Jews out of 12 million. But today the Jews rule this world by proxy. They get others to fight and die for them."

—A speech by the prime minister of Malaysia, Dr. Mahathir Mohamad, at the opening of the biggest summit of Muslims in three years at the Islamic Summit Conference in Malaysia during the fall of 2003. He said that most of the Western leaders are biased against Muslims and wanted to recolonize them.

"The Defense Department informed me in writing six months ago that it was launching a review to determine whether changes need to be made in the groups we rely on to train Muslim ministers and whether a violent form of Islam is being preached in the military. So it's shocking that the Defense Department has been silent on this issue and is now issuing public comments that no such examination is underway."

—United States Senator Charles Schumer's comments in light of a Muslim military chaplain being held on possible relations to terrorist groups.

"Anyone concerned with what's happening in our world ought to spend some time reading the Koran."

—Andy Rooney, the CBS commentator, gave this advice shortly after September 11, 2001. Mohammed Atta, one of the suicide terrorists of September 11, had a Qur'an in his suitcase as he checked it for the ill-doomed flight. He also had a five-page document with advice for his fellow hijackers to recite the Qur'an. In the weeks after September 11, the largest publisher of the Qur'an in the United States reported sales had quintupled. It had to airlift copies from Great Britain to meet the demand. American bookstores reported selling more Qur'ans than Bibles.

"We're not attacking Islam but Islam has attacked us. The God of Islam is not the same God. He's not the Son of God of

the Christian or Judeo-Christian faith. It's a different God, and I believe it is a very evil and wicked religion."
—Franklin Graham, October 2001 http://www.cnsnews. com/ViewCulture.asp?Page=%5CCulture%5Carchive%5C2001 11%5CCUL20011122b.html.

We do believe Islam is at war with the Christian West."
—Paul Weyrich and William S. Lind, reported by Wes Vernon, 9 May 2002] http://www.newsmax.com/archives/ articles/2002/5/8/183305.shtml

"Christianity was founded by the virgin-born Jesus Christ. Islam was founded by Mohammed, a demon-possessed pedophile who had 12 wives, and his last one was a 9-year-old girl.
"Allah is not Jehovah, either. Jehovah is not going to turn anyone into a terrorist that will try to bomb people and take the lives of thousands and thousands of people."
—Jerry Vines, 14 June 2002http://www.biblicalrecorder.org/ content/news/2002/6_14_2002/ne140602vines.shtml.

"Some of the comments that have been uttered about Islam do not reflect the sentiments of my government or the sentiments of most Americans. Ours is a country based on tolerance."
—President Bush, 13 November 2002 http://usembassy. state.gov/tokyo/wwwhsoc20021118a1.html.

"I want everybody to understand that one disagreement, a minor disagreement among friends does not end a friendship; and so I'm not one throwing rocks at the President. I appreciate the President, appreciate what he's doing; and I want everybody to know that something like this does not sever the support that I have given to him over the years. However, I want to clarify something. The purest expression of Islam in the world is found among the Wahabi sect of Saudi Arabia, and that sect pretty much dominates the religious life of Saudi Arabia and has been the fountainhead for the terrorists. The Wahabis in turn have established a pure Islamic state in Afghanistan, and the group in charge of that was called the Taliban. The other pure Islamic state that we're familiar with is in Iran, where the Ayatollah Khomeini came in, and the word, [*Ayat Allah*] means 'the spirit of Allah.' He was establishing a pure, Islamic state. Now this state was characterized by our President as part of an 'axis of evil.' The other state that I'm aware of that is a pure Islamic state is Sudan where Sharia is practiced and at least 2.5 million Christians have been killed. Now having said that, there is no doubt that the religion of Mohammed and those who adhere to

Dr. Braswell's Class Visiting Islamic Mosque in Washington, DC

it firmly, such as the Wahabis, and the Taliban and the Iranian Mullahs and other Mullahs operating in other parts of the world, is extreme and violent. However, we must distinguish between the origin of the religion and the adherents to it in the United States who indeed are peaceful people. So to say 'the religion is peaceful' I don't think is accurate. To say that most of the adherents in America to the Islamic faith are peaceful is absolutely correct. It's just a question of semantics, but I think we ought to get the semantics clear."

—Pat Robertson, 14 November 2002 http://www. patrobertson.com/PressReleases/bushresponse3.asp.

"Today, we lack metrics to know if we are winning or losing the global war on terror. Are we capturing, killing or deterring and dissuading more terrorists every day than the madrasas and the radical clerics are recruiting, training and deploying against us? Does the U.S. need to fashion a broad, integrated plan to stop the next generation of terrorists?"

—Donald Rumsfeld ["Leaked Memo" of 16 October 2003] http://www.foxnews.com/story/0,2933,100917,00.html.

"We must embark on a major initiative of public diplomacy to bridge the divide between Islam and the rest of the world. We must make avoidance of the clash of civilizations the work of our generation: Engaging in a new effort to bring to the table a new face of the Arab world—Muslim clerics, mullahs, imams and secular leaders—demonstrating for the entire world a peaceful religion which can play an enormous role in isolating and rebutting those practitioners who would pervert Islam's true message."

—John Kerry, 23 December 2003 http://www.us-israel.org/ jsource/US-Israel/kerry.html.

"We have been talking not only to the Saudis, but to other Middle Eastern leaders and Muslim leaders around the world, and made it clear to them that Islam is a great religion. But they also have to be educating their youngsters not just in the tenets of Islam and the Islamic religion, but they have to educate their youngsters for the demands of the 21st century. They've got to give them skills. They've got to teach them to read and write. They've got to teach them Science and Math and all the other things that are necessary for societies to be successful in the 21st century.

"And if they're just going to take their young people and put them in these madrasas, these schools that do nothing but indoctrinate them in the worst aspects of a religion, then they are shorting themselves, they are leaving themselves back as well as teaching hatred that will not help us bring peace to the region, and will not help their societies. And we're working on them on—in this regard. We have the Middle East Partnership Initiative. We're helping them to learn how to educate youngsters for the 21st century. And I think that the President has made it clear that democracy is not just a political form of government for the West. It can apply to any nation, any society; no matter what the religion is. And why shouldn't it apply to these democracies that'll work best in the 21st century?"

—Colin Powell Interview with Michael Smerconish on 21 January 2004] http://www.state.gov/secretary/rm/28292.htm.

APPENDIX 2

As Muhammad Says, Muhammad Does

Muslims honor Muhammad and follow his counsel. They believe he was the final prophet with the perfect truth from Allah.

Some non-Muslims think he was the greatest religious figure of all time. Other non-Muslims from Martin Luther to contemporary preachers castigate him as the antichrist, a false prophet, and a pedophile.

Some things are most certain about Muhammad.

Muhammad (AD 570–632) was born in the city of Mecca, which is in present Saudi Arabia. He founded the religion, Islam. In the first one hundred years after his death, Islam spread faster than any religion in history. Today it has over 1.3 billion followers and is the majority religion in over forty nations.

Muhammad was a premier leader. He combined the roles of prophet, patriarch, politician, judge, and commander-in-chief to establish a powerfully emerging Islamic empire under the rule of Allah and himself and his successors.

Muhammad was decisive in his leadership. When the Jewish tribes refused to submit to his orders, he led his militia to slaughter the males and take the women as concubines.

He practiced the art of diplomacy. When Jews and Christians refused to become Muslims, he treated them as "People of the Book." They could have their synagogues and churches with certain restrictions as long as they submitted to Islamic authority and rule and paid the taxes.

Muhammad was a warrior. His vision included peace for all under the truthful and authentic rule of Islam. He urged Muslims to take up martyrdom in jihad against the enemies of Islam with its immediate reward in paradise.

He was a family man. At the age of twenty-five, he married Khadijah, a wealthy widow merchant who was forty years old. After her death he learned from Allah that he could have more than the maximum of four wives provided for males from the Quran. Thus, Muhammad, with this exception, took widows and concubines and other females to live in his harem. The last wife, Aisha, was his favorite. They were engaged when she was six years old and consummated their marriage when she was nine.

Muhammad preached on many topics: helping the poor and needy, being honest in commerce, and being regular in prayer, fasting, and the worship of Allah.

Today, the name of Allah is heard around the globe. Islam is one of the fastest-growing religions. The name of Muhammad is given to tens of thousands of newborn Muslim boys.

Muslims daily pray, "There is no god but Allah, and Muhammad is the prophet of Allah." He is their inspiration, their example, and their guidance.

The Christian who looks at Muhammad and Islam is reminded of Jesus riding on the back of a donkey into Jerusalem during his last days, not triumphantly on the back of a warrior's stallion. One is reminded of Jesus telling the disciple to put up his sword and not use it against the enemies who came to apprehend him in the Garden of Gethsemane. One is reminded of Jesus' words on the cross: "Father, forgive them for they know not what they do."

As Muhammad says, Muhammad does. Islam has come a long way because of this warrior's decisions, power, and influence in the religious, political, and social lives of nations. Today there are 1.3 billion Muslims.

Militancy and Martyrdom in Islam: Peace and War

Since the terrorist attack on September 11, 2001, Americans have asked, "Why would any Muslim do such a thing?" Is there something in Islam that promotes physical militancy and violence?

President Bush spoke of Islam as a peaceful religion. Muslim leaders asserted that the acts of the terrorists were not representative of Islam. Observers noted that most of the world's Muslims live in peace with their neighbors.

What sense can one make of a senseless act by nineteen hijackers of four planes that resulted in the deaths of thousands of people, especially since later evidence revealed that they did this in the name of Allah and on the basis of their religion Islam?

Islam is a peaceful religion. Muslims believe that Allah is a compassionate and merciful God. Islam's sacred book teaches good relations with one's neighbors.

Islam is also a fourteen-hundred-year-old religion with a history of warfare, violence, and militancy against its neighbors, tribes, and nations. In recent history Islamic sectarianism of Wahabism in Saudi Arabia has informed the mind and heart of Osama bin Laden, who has inspired many Muslims to go on jihad against many enemies, including Jews, Christians, and anyone who sides with the enemy.

Ayatollah Khomeini, after establishing the Islamic Republic of Iran, fought an eight-year war against neighboring Iraq that inspired hundreds of thousands of youth to sacrifice their lives as martyrs because of the promise of paradise immediately after dying in battle for Allah. For some twenty years Khomeini exported his Islamic militancy and martyrdom to various parts of the Middle East, Asia, and Africa.

What, then, are the sources in Islam for teaching and promoting militancy and martyrdom? Islam's three major sources are the Qur'an (the sacred scripture), the Hadith (the sayings and deeds of Muhammad that serve as examples for all Muslims), and the Shar'ia (the developed laws and traditions that inform Muslim behavior).

The Qur'an contains many verses calling Muslims to kill and do violence to the enemies of Allah. The Hadith gives many statements and examples of the prophet Muhammad as he commanded the death of others, as he led warriors into battle to kill individuals and tribes and as he promised paradise to martyrs for the cause of Allah. The Shar'ia is a complex tradition of laws that sets forth the principles and methods of warfare to determine its legitimate causes and how it may be waged.

Islam is a religion based on a high view of its authority, of its superiority as a system not only of religion but of principles of politics, economics, social behavior, family, hygiene, and relations to peoples such as the Jews, Christians, and other religionists.

Where Islam is predominant among a population, usually there are minorities who are given certain rights and privileges within the governance of Islamic authorities. History has demonstrated that when a Muslim opts to join another religion, that one is declared an apostate and serious consequences prevail such as persecution, excommunication from family and community, or death.

Americans still ask if Islam is a peaceful religion. They also ask why there is such violence taught or allowed by Islamic leaders. Militancy and martyrdom continue to be a focus of attention. Many Muslims are concerned with these questions also.

Do We Outsiders Really Know Iraq and Iran and Shiite and Sunni Muslims?

What does history tell us about Islam, especially the strained and aggrevating relations between Sunni and Shiite Muslims? Why has Iran—a nation more than 90 percent Muslim, and a non-Arab one at that—looked with suspicion and distrust at other Sunni Muslim Arab nations and even fought an eight-year war with Iraq?

Why had many Shiites rather go to sacred Shiite sites in Kerbala and Nejaf, Iraq, and to Meshad, Iran, than to the holy pilgrimage site in Mecca, Saudi Arabia? Why have the majority Shiites in Iraq been under attack by the minority Sunni population for decades, and what have been the aspirations of the Iraqi Shiites who in any election would outnumber the Iraqi Sunnis?

I taught Iranian Shiite clergy for over five years as professor of English and comparative religions at the Faculty of Islamic Theology of the University of Teheran, Iran. I visited tens and tens of their mosques, heard numerous sermons from the ayatollahs, and engaged Shiites in the marketplace, as well as in the mosques and homes in lengthy conversations.

In a nutshell, both Sunni and Shiite Muslims, wherever they live, are required by Islam and the Qu'ran to believe and practice the following with little if any differences: There is one God named Allah; Muhammad is the final prophet; the Qu'ran is the last and perfect revelation from Allah; there is a judgment day where one will either be judged to paradise or to hell; one must say five stated prayers each day facing Mecca; one must give certain percentages of income and property to Islamic institutions; one must fast during the month of Ramadan; one must take a pilgrimage (hajj) to Mecca once in a lifetime if able financially and if healthy. And one should be engaged in jihad, the struggle to be a good Muslim and to establish the superior religion, Islam.

Shiites, however, deviate from the orthodoxy of the above beliefs and practices to which the Sunnis adhere. The historical disconnect from the Sunnis occurred when Muhammad died and his son-in-law, Ali, claimed successorship to the leadership of Muhammad. The traditionalists, the Sunnis, denied Ali's claim and elected their leaders. Thus, the Sunni caliphate developed versus the Shiite imamate.

The schism between the Sunnis and the Shiites was intensified after the Sunni army killed Ali's son and Muhammad's grandson, Husain, at the battle in Kerbala, Iraq in AD 680 Husain had claimed to be the leader of all Muslims. The Sunni army slaughtered all but a few of Husain's family and followers. Husain was beheaded, his body mutilated, and his head was paraded back in the streets of Damascus, Syria, where the Sunni caliphate presided.

Not only have the Shiite imams developed a leadership different from that of the Sunni caliphs, but they also have developed a different theology and practice. They believe that twelve imams succeeded one another and that the twelfth imam will return to restore righteousnes and justice in the world. They direct their intercessory prayer to figures like Ali and Husain. They visit tombs and imamzadehs to offer prayers and gifts to the saints and heroes of the Shiite faith.

They celebrate the season of Muharram with sermons and addresses, plays and street marches, remembering tragedy at

Kerbala and Husain's violent death at the hands of the Sunnis. Millions of Shiites cry, grieve, and curse the infidel Sunnis. Men, especially, march in the streets beating their chests with chains and drawing blood on their white outer garments.

I have heard sermons and addresses in their mosques and homes and seen the marches with bright red blood spewing onto their white clothes. I have seen women cry and men shout their anger at the Sunnis.

What should we outsiders make of all this?

1. History is important to Sunnis and Shiites, and they remember it well.

2. Much of the history of Islamic beginnings, as well as recent happenings, is bathed in violence, bloodshed, and schism.

3. Sunnis consider the Shittes as deviants, or even heretics, from traditional, orthodox Islam.

4. Shiites remember the brutality and violence of the Sunnis against Ali and Husain, Muhammad's son-in-law and grandson. Shiite history, memory, ceremonies, rituals, beliefs, and practices aggravate suspicion, distrust, and animosity toward Sunnis.

5. Recent history records the eight-year war of Khomeini's Shiite Iran against Iraq in which hundreds of thousands of Sunnis and Shiites were killed.

6. The recent history of Iraq records the dominance of the Sunni minority and often the punishment of the Shiite majority.

7. Saudi Arabia, the near neighbor of Iraq and Iran, under the radical and militant Wahabi Sunni Muslims, despises the Shiites and considers them not only deviants from true Islam but infidels.

8. Both the Wahabi Sunni Islam and the Sunni Islam of Osama bin Laden and his followers and the Shiite Islam of Ayatollah Khomeini and his present descendants in Iran all think they have the superior Islam for themselves and for the globe. They also think that non-Muslims and particularly

certain westerners, and especially the United States, are the "Great Satan" and infidels.

9. The Shiites will have their own agenda in Iraq based on their history, their view of Sunnis, and their aspirations to bring Shiite theology and practice to fruition.

10. Islam has considered Christians as a part of a scriptural tradition who should have respect and should be protected by Islamic authorities. Islam completely rejects, however, the Christian teachings of Jesus as the Son of God, as crucified on the cross and risen from the grave, and as the bringer and giver of salvation.

We outsiders know little of the religions, cultures, and politics of Islam and the Sunnis and the Shiites. American foreign policy may be based on ideals of democracy and liberty and freedom, but the cultural heroes of Sunnis and Shiites march to different drummers.

Christians may be aware of their study of and relationships, especially with Shiites, of their longing for more "personal" relations in their religion with intercessory prayers to their "saints" and heroes like Ali and Husain, of their offerings and supplications at the tombs of their religious heroes, and of their cries and bloodletting to Husain and the twelfth imam to do something about their injustices and their poverty and despair. Evidently, the Shiites feel that Allah may just be too far away to assist in these personal and heart and earthly matters.

Admittedly, Sunnis and Shiites have complexities in their religions. Outsiders must avoid simplistic answers. Outsiders such as Christians and Americans must learn more about the history, cultures, and religious aspirations of Sunnis and Shiites. They all affect us.

The Islamic Republic of North America?

Ayatollah Khomeini, Osama bin Laden, and the Wahabi sect of Saudi Arabia agree that Allah has ordained Islam as the superior religion for all humanity.

The blueprint for implementing the superior religion Islam is found in the inerrant and infallible Qur'an, in the sayings and traditions of the Muslim prophet Muhammad, and in the Sharia and Sunna of Islamic caliphs and ulema over the fourteen hundred years of Islamic caliphates, empires, and cultures.

Islam sharply distinguishes between two worlds: the enlightened world governed by Islam and the darkened world governed by the ignorant, the corrupt, the immoral, and the non-submitters to Allah.

Islam, the superior religion, promotes belief in monotheism, angels, prophets, holy scriptures, and the last days of judgment with resolution of destiny to paradise or hell.

Islam promotes the superior practices: worship of only one deity Allah, guidance of his final prophet Muhammad, basic financial contributions for the upkeep and spread of Islam, daily prayers facing Mecca, fasting during Ramadan each year, pilgrimage once in a lifetime to Mecca, and jihad to spread and defend Islam.

Islam reviles atheism, condemns Christianity as blasphemy, and lashes out against secularism. Jews and Christians are "people of scripture" who have become corrupt in their teach-

Islamic Center of Raleigh, NC

ings and cultures and need conversion to Islam. Where Islam has dominated political authority and power, non-Muslims have faced limited toleration and often persecution.

In order to bring the world to accept the faith, Islam has implemented the practice of jihad. It has two meanings. The first meaning is to persuade, invite, educate, and train non-Muslims to accept the superior religion. The other meaning is to defend Islam when it is attacked by others by declaring a jihad of military or violent means to defeat the enemy.

Islam has grown to some 1.3 billion adherents and is found in most cultures around the globe. It has grown by encouraging large families. "Once a Muslim always a Muslim" is the teaching of Islam. Anyone who leaves Islam is declared an apostate.

Islamic mosques and schools (madrasa) dot the landscape from Saudi Arabia to Pakistan and from Iran eastward. They are spread across many parts of Africa and are now spreading in Europe and North America. They teach that Islam is a superior system of religion, politics, and culture. They also revile and castigate the blasphemous cultures and peoples of non-Muslims, especially of Jews, Christians, and Americans.

Ayatollah Khomeini labeled America as "the Great Satan," declared a jihad against the novelist Salman Rushdie, author of *The Satanic Verses,* and spent much of Iran's oil money to export Islam across the world and to fund the militant Hizbollah against Israel.

The Wahabi Islamic teachings of the Saudi Arabian ulema in their mosques and schools and writings lambast non-Muslims and seek to extend their interpretation of Islam across cultures and lands, using the oil wealth of the Saudi royalty. Their teachings have influenced Muslim thinkers in Egypt, Pakistan, and India, as well as Osama bin Laden.

Osama bin Laden in his thinking, writings, and actions has promoted Islam as the superior religion, has denigrated Jews and Christians as corrupt and blasphemers, and has labeled the United States and Muslim rulers he considers illegitimate as targets of jihad. Americans are to be targets of jihad wherever they are found around the world.

The common theme throughout this common vision is that Islam is superior, that Allah and Islam have been attacked, and that Muslims must not only declare jihad against these enemies but also launch attacks against them wherever they are found and by whatever means of violence may be appropriate and feasible for the circumstances.

African-American Mosque
in Washington, DC

Mosque in Alma Ata, Kazakhstan
Built by Saudi Arabia

APPENDIX 6

What the Qur'an Says

About Itself

An inspired message (4:82; 6:19)
God's revelation (6:92; 7:105–107); 27:6; 45:2)
Revelation in Arabic (12:2; 13:37; 41:44; 42:7; 43:30; 16:103)
A tablet preserved (85:21–22; 43:1–4; 13:39)
Relation to unbelievers (17:45–47; 84:20–25)
Same message to earlier prophets (41:43; 43:44–45)
Instruction, good news, warnings (17:9–10; 31:3; 6:155)

About Allah

Oneness (112:1–4)
Partnership with Allah a grave sin (4:48)
Names (59:22–24)
Satanic verses (53:19–23; 22:51–53)

About Islamic Beliefs and Practices

Angels (2:285; 6:100; 34:40–41; 46:29–32; 72:1–28)
Prophets (2:38, 177, 252, 285; 4:80, 164; 18:110; 10:48; 16:36; 40:15)
Day of judgment and resurrection (55; 4:45; 14:16–17; 53:31)
Great confession or creed (3:81; 5:83–84;)
Required prayers (2:3, 177; 11:114; 17:78; 30:17–18)
Required almsgiving (2:43, 83, 110, 177, 277; 9:60)
Required fasting (Ramadan): 2:183–185)
Required pilgrimage (2:196–201; 3:97; 22:26–29)

About Jihad

Individual struggle and community warfare (2:244; 9:5; 9:29; 22:78; 47:4; 49:15

Martyrdom (shahid) 47:4–5

To vindicate a wrong (22:40)

With goods and lives and a promise of reward to those killed (3:157–8, 169–172)

Threat if one does not fight with severe punishments in the hereafter (9:81–82)

Allah says to fight but not to agree (2:129)

To fight leaders of unbelief (9:13)

To fight unbelievers until they pay tribute out of hand and have been humbled (9:5, 29)

Required even for those who dislike fighting (2:216)

About Freedom of Religion

No compulsion in religion (2:256)

Islam the only religion (3:85)

About Jesus, Christians, and Jews

Jesus born of virgin Mary (chapter 3)

Jesus the Messiah (3:45)

Jesus only a messenger (4:171; 5:75)

Jesus a prophet (19:30)

Jesus the word and spirit of Allah (4:171)

Jesus' miracles (3:49; 5:110)

Denial of Jesus as Son of God (3:42–47; 112)

Denial of Jesus and the Trinity (5:73; 116)

Denial of Jesus' crucifixion (4:156–158)

Jesus raised up to God (3:48–55; 4:156–157; 19:33–34)

The gospel (3:3–4; 57:27; 5:48)

Christians and Jews as people of the book (3:64–80; 29:46; 5:48; 5:82–86)

Selected Reading List

Abdalati, Hammudah. *Islam in Focus.* Indianapolis: American Trust Publications, 1975.

Ali, Abullah Yusuf. *The Meaning of the Holy Qur'an:* New Edition with Revised Translation and Commentary. Brentwood, Md.: Amana Corporation, 1989.

Braswell, George W., Jr. *Islam: Its Prophet, Peoples, Politics, and Power.* Nashville: Broadman & Holman Publishers, 1996.

_____ *What You Need to Know about Islam.* Nashville: Broadman & Holman Publishers, 2000.

Cragg, Kenneth. *Muhammad and the Christian.* Marynoll: Orbis Books, 1984.

_____ The *Arab Christian: A History in the Middle East.* Louisville: Westminster/John Knox Press, 1991.

Esposito, John L. *The Oxford Encyclopeida of the Modern Islamic World.* 4 Volumes. New York: Oxford University Press, 1995.

Huntington, Samuel. *The Clash of Civilizations and the Remaking of World Order.* New York: Simon and Schuster, 1996.

Kelsay, John. *Islam and War: A Study in Comparative Ethics, the Gulf War and Beyond.* Louisville: Westminster/John Knox Press, 1993.

Khomeini, Ayatollah. *Islamic Government.* New York: Manor Books, 1979.

Lewis, Bernard. "The Roots of Muslim Rage," *The Atlantic Monthly,* September 1990.

_____ *What Went Wrong?* New York: Oxford University Press, 2002.

Lincoln, Eric. *The Black Muslims in America*. Grand Rapids: Eerdmans, 1994.

Mohammad, Nazar, compiler. *Commandments by God in the Quran*. New York: The Message Publications, 1991.

Naipaul, V. S. *Beyond Belief: Islamic Excursions Among the Converted Peoples*. New York: Random House, 1998.

Parrinder, Geoffrey. *Jesus in the Qur'an*. New York: Oxford University Press, 1997.

Watt, W. Montgomery. *Muslim-Christian Encounters*. London: Routledge, 1991.

Zepp, Ira. *A Muslim Primer*. Westminster: Wakefield Edition, 1992.